BOOK I

ENGLISH IN CONTEXT

Reading Comprehension
for Science and Technology

Joan M. Saslow

John F. Mongillo

Prentice-Hall, Inc., Englewood Cliffs, New Jersey   07632

Library of Congress Cataloging in Publication Data

Saslow, Joan M.   (date)
    English in context.

SEP 1 6 1986

    1. English language—Text-books for foreign speakers.
2. English language—Technical English.   3. College
readers.   4. Readers—Science.   5. Readers—Technology.
I. Mongillo, John F.   II. Title.
PE1128.S274   1985   428.6'4'0245   84-4800
ISBN   0-13-280025-X

Editorial/production supervision and
        interior design: Barbara Alexander
Cover design: Whitman Studio, Inc.
Photo research: Teri Stratford
Manufacturing buyer: Harry P. Baisley

Cover photo credit: Courtesy Strippit-Houdaille, Akron, N.Y.
Lesson opening photo credits:

1: General Motors; 2: Courtesy Strippit-Houdaille, Akron, N.Y.; 3: U.S. Geological
Survey, Department of the Interior; 4: USDA Photo by Doug Wilson; 5: Richard
Ellis, Photo Researchers, Inc.; 6: Andre La Roche, Energy Conversion Devices, Inc.;
7: NASA; 8: United Nations; 9: NASA; 10: Japanese National Railways

Printed in the United States of America

10   9   8   7   6   5   4   3   2   1

ISBN 0-13-280025-X   01

PRENTICE-HALL INTERNATIONAL, INC., *London*
PRENTICE-HALL OF AUSTRALIA PTY. LIMITED, *Sydney*
EDITORA PRENTICE-HALL DO BRASIL, LTDA., *Rio de Janeiro*
PRENTICE-HALL OF CANADA, LTD., *Toronto*
PRENTICE-HALL OF INDIA PRIVATE LIMITED, *New Delhi*
PRENTICE-HALL OF JAPAN, INC., *Tokyo*
PRENTICE-HALL OF SOUTHEAST ASIA PTE. LTD., *Singapore*
WHITEHALL BOOKS LIMITED, *Wellington, New Zealand*

Contents

Preface

Purpose

English in Context: Reading Comprehension for Science and Technology is an intermediate-level reading comprehension text series for students who want concentrated practice in reading scientific and technical English. The sole purpose of this three-level text series is to build the comprehension skill. Although it is unarguably true that listening, speaking, and writing practice enhance the reading skill, practice in reading itself is a more direct route to this goal. Thus, *English in Context: Reading Comprehension for Science and Technology* elicits no production of written or spoken English, and includes no listening comprehension activities. Students at the intermediate level may already have been exposed to years of classroom practice of "the four skills." What is provided here, then, is an alternate path focused entirely on reading.

Student Profile

English in Context: Reading Comprehension for Science and Technology is intended for students who have had beginning-level courses in English, either at the secondary-school level or at the university, the technical school, or the binational institute. These students typically have had two- to three-hundred hours of classroom instruction, often in large classes. They have been exposed, at one time or another (and with greater or lesser amounts of success), to the "basic structures" of the language, and they have a fair vocabulary covering everyday activities, work, school, play, and hobbies. They function conversationally at a low level and make many mistakes in grammar, lexicon, and pronunciation. They understand more difficult language than that which they can produce on their own. Their reading ability generally corresponds to what they can say, because they have studied from texts that "strictly control" the reading narratives. These students approach all unfamiliar readings with a bilingual dictionary close at hand, since they are unskilled in deriving meaning from passages containing new words without translating every new word into their own language. They are particularly handicapped when facing a scientific or technical reading because their training has been in "everyday" English. It should be kept in mind that the students for whom these three texts in the *English in Context* series were created are not English majors, but rather are specialists (or specialists in training) in some area of science or technology.

Scope of the Series

English in Context: Reading Comprehension for Science and Technology Books 1 and 2 are similar in design and format (described below), while Book 3 differs significantly. Since the purpose of the series as a whole is to prepare students to read authentic published source materials in any area of science or technology, the first two books concentrate on reading selections especially written to ready students for this goal by illustrating the use of high-frequency science vocabulary and important concepts in grammar and syntax. Book 3, on the other hand, has been designed to bridge the gap between the "engineered" reading selections of Books 1 and 2 and free reading, in that it centers on real, unedited excerpts from published science textbooks and journals while maintaining a good deal of supporting exercise and explanatory material.

Working Assumptions

Underlying the development of these materials are several assumptions. The first is that scientific and technical English are English. The characteristic features of this type of writing are all found in all other forms of English. Colin R. Elliot has remarked that [except for technical terms and some more complex structures] "there is little to distinguish it from any other form of writing which seeks to explain and exemplify general theories or describe processes" (ELT Journal, October 1976). J. D. Corbluth (ELT Journal, July 1975) even disagrees that there is such a thing as scientific English at all. Although other possible grammatical frameworks exist (notably Ewer's Microacts, for example), we have chosen to base these materials on the assumption that the similarities between scientific/technical English and ordinary English are greater than the differences between them, always recognizing, however, that students predictably will have difficulty with certain syntactical and grammatical features which occur frequently. Some well-recognized examples of these are passive voice, noun compounds, *if*-clauses, long preposed modifying clusters, and reduced adjective clauses. These have been given particular emphasis.

In addition to the choice of the syntactical and grammatical features in each lesson, certain words were chosen for inclusion in the vocabulary sections at the beginning of each lesson. It is our working assumption that most of these words are probably not known by the student who has had the two- to three-hundred hours of English described above. These words are found over and over in scientific and technical prose. Most of them are of a type we call "subtechnical," that is, they are not highly specialized for one narrow field of interest but rather are found in writings in all areas of science and technology. It is our belief that knowing these words will greatly increase comprehension of scientific and technical narrative. These words are further and more specifically described below under Vocabulary.

"Vocabulary of ideas" is another category of words included in the Vocabulary section at the beginning of each lesson. These words are not really "science" or "technology" words at all but rather are used frequently to express concepts and ideas in the type of writing students will be reading. It must be admitted, however, that the inclusion of some words under one or the other rubric is sometimes debatable and concededly made on a subjective, and sometimes almost arbitrary, basis. The major value of having the vocabulary divided into two parts is to "lighten the load" of words to be learned at one time. We chose to distinguish these two gross categories of words in the belief that some of the vocabulary, though not at all "scientific" or "technical" (such as *predominantly*), are used with extremely high frequency in scientific and technical prose. Furthermore, we felt that these words differ in a general way from more strictly "scientific" or "technical" words, such as, for example, *buoyancy*. Although this distinction is very clear for these two examples, we must recognize that the choice of placement for all words is not always that evident.

Organization and Lesson Format

Each lesson in *English in Context: Reading Comprehension for Science and Technology* is built around a reading selection on a timely scientific or technical topic. *All other sections of the lesson are tightly connected to the reading, either as a preparation for it or an extension of it.* In this way, *every* word and *every* exercise deals with comprehension of the central reading selection of the lesson.

VOCABULARY*

The vocabulary section that appears at the beginning of each lesson is made up of Subtechnical Vocabulary, Vocabulary of Ideas, and, occasionally, Thought Connectors. Each lesson presents twenty to thirty important new words.

Subtechnical Vocabulary. Some examples are *retractable, fuel, deposit, devise, stress, yield, trait, field, breakthrough, dwindle, resource, equip, standardize,* and *retrieval.* Almost all these words will be found sooner or later in students' independent reading, regardless of their specialized interests. Each word is defined in the limited sense in which it is used in the reading selection to follow. The word is then presented in a simple contextual sentence which further conveys and fixes its meaning. Where necessary or helpful, an illustration is also provided as a meaning conveyor.

*Note: *All* vocabulary in these sections is used in the reading selection to come.

Vocabulary of Ideas. These words and expressions are also taken from the reading selection to follow and are less technical *per se* than the words described previously. (For the rationale for the division between "subtechnical vocabulary" and "vocabulary of ideas," see Working Assumptions, page viii.) Some examples of such words are *overcome, involve, account for, subject to, supply, buildup, level, marginal, feasibility, alternate, outlook, depend on,* and *potential.* As with the Subtechnical Vocabulary, each word is defined and used in a contextual sentence.

Thought Connectors. When included, these rhetorical items are essential connectors of ideas in scientific and technical writing. Some examples are *therefore, consequently, furthermore, in spite of,* and *nevertheless.* As with the Subtechnical Vocabulary and the Vocabulary of Ideas, the goal is comprehension—not production—of these words.

Vocabulary Exercises. It is every language teacher's experience that in order to make vocabulary "active," rigorous practice is necessary. All too often at the intermediate level, students' vocabularies stop growing because it is assumed that practice is only appropriate for beginners. A series of exercises in each of these lessons provides students with yet another opportunity to see each of the vocabulary words from that lesson in a relevant contextual sentence. These exercises are not a test. They are meant to help commit meaning to memory. Not only will each word be elicited as an answer to a question, but it also will be used several other times in items eliciting other vocabulary words as answers.

COMPREHENSION SKILL INDEX (Skills and Syntactical-Grammatical Concepts)

Before and after the reading selection in each lesson, facsimiles of index cards signal the names of comprehension skills or important grammatical or syntactical concepts presented in that lesson. These skills and topics comprise the comprehension index. Some of the skills are skimming, scanning, reading comprehension, confirming content, understanding vocabulary from context, understanding vocabulary from word parts, and drawing conclusions. Syntactical and grammatical topics include noun compounds, passive voice, *if*-clauses, preposed modifying clusters, and gerunds. Throughout, great care has been taken to select the teaching approach best suited to building *comprehension rather than production* of the various syntactical and grammatical concepts. A brief example is the treatment of *if*-clauses in Lesson Eight. Texts concerned with production of this structure give practice in the sequence of tenses to use in both clauses of sentences expressing contrary-to-fact ideas as well as in sentences that express real conditions. Here, on the other hand, the explanatory copy points out that *if*-clause sentences in the present tense express facts and beliefs; those using *will* express predictions; those using *would* express probable outcomes of conditions not presently existing; and those using *would have, could have, might have,* and *should have* express what could have happened in the past under conditions that did not exist. *English in Context: Reading Comprehension for Science and Technology* provides no practice in usage of these structures, but only in deriving meaning from sentences that use them. Consequently, the exercises ask the students to choose explanations for sentences in the reading using *if*-clauses. In addition, students do intensive work with the reading selection in that lesson, making sure they can comprehend the grammatical or syntactical concept at hand. The reading selection has, in fact, been written specifically to use the targeted syntax or grammar concept numerous times. In Lesson One, for example, noun compounds are presented. The reading selection in that lesson contains no fewer than twenty-six of these noun compounds.

Comprehension Skill Index Exercises. In each section of the comprehension index, exercises are provided. It is important to note that no production of the targeted concepts is necessary in these exercises. Rather, students receive practice in deriving meaning from sentences containing the targeted concepts. All sentences used in these exercises come from the reading selection, providing cross reinforcement of each concept.

READING SELECTION

The reading selection is the core of each lesson and the source of all the vocabulary, comprehension index skills, and syntax and grammar topics presented in that lesson. Each reading concerns an exciting subject designed to be of interest to any modern reader who has a basic knowledge of science and who lives in today's world. A glance at the titles of these selections in the Table of Contents will make this apparent. Care has also been taken in ensuring that the instructor with a humanities rather than a science background will be comfortable teaching these selections.

The readings get linguistically more complex, conceptually denser, and rhetorically more sophisticated as each book develops. As previously pointed out, each reading uses numerous examples of the syntactical and grammatical concepts targeted in that lesson. In addition, each of the vocabulary words that appeared in the vocabulary section at the beginning of the lesson appears at least once in the reading selection. These vocabulary words can be easily spotted, as they are set in boldface type, reminding the student to notice these important words once more in the context of the reading selection.

The side notes that appear alongside the reading define words that most students probably do not know. These words are less essential for a student's active vocabulary because of their lower frequency in scientific and technical writing. However, some of these words should be considered active vocabulary by specialists in the particular field dealt with in the reading. An example of such a word is *birthmark,* in Lesson Two. Any student whose main interest is medicine—or particularly dermatology—will find this to be an important word. Most other students will not; for this reason birthmark was not included in the Subtechnical Vocabulary at the beginning of the lesson but instead is side noted alongside its occurrence in the reading.

JOAN M. SASLOW
JOHN F. MONGILLO

LESSON ONE

Aerodynamics in Car Design

An engineer checks drag coefficient numbers in the test section control room of the wind tunnel.

Subtechnical Vocabulary

full-size (adjective)

> standard-size; normally big
>
> **Full-size** cars use more gas than smaller cars.

streamlined (adjective)

> designed for speed and easy movement
>
> The new trains are all **streamlined** and much faster than the older trains.

streamlined

retractable (adjective)

> capable of being pulled in so that it cannot be seen
>
> Many pens have **rectractable** points.

retractable point

force (noun)

> physical power, energy, strength
>
> Gravity is the **force** that holds us close to the earth.

resistance (noun)

opposition of one thing to another

A parachute offers **resistance** to the wind.

fuel (noun)

material that is burned to provide power or heat

Wood, oil, coal, and gas are **fuels**.

ratio (noun)

numerical relation between two related things

The **ratio** of cars to trucks on this road is three to one.

width (noun)

distance from one side to the other side of an object

This book has a **width** of 15 centimeters.

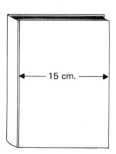

15 cm.

vacuum (noun)

> the empty space that occurs when all air is taken away; a completely empty space
>
> When all the air is taken from a container a **vacuum** occurs.

model (noun)

> a smaller representation of a full-size object
>
> Architects make **models** of the buildings they design.

to check (verb)

> to look at; to investigate; to test; to measure
>
> The man **checked** the thermometer to see what the temperature was.

to reduce (verb)

> to make smaller, to lessen
>
> Cold **reduces** the volume of gases.

to indicate (verb)

> to show
>
> The speedometer **indicates** how fast the car is traveling.

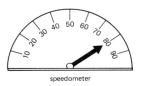

speedometer

to install (verb)

> to put in a position for use
>
> An electrician **installs** new electrical wiring.

Vocabulary of Ideas

to overcome (verb)

> to win against

> Antibodies help us **to overcome** infection.

to encounter (verb)

> to find

> We **encounter** new ideas whenever we travel to new places.

to involve (verb)

> to require; to include

> Science **involves** the study of physics, chemistry, and biology.

to account for (phrasal verb)

> to explain; to cause

> Good care **accounts for** the larger size of this plant.

to cut down on (phrasal verb)

> to reduce

> It is necessary **to cut down on** calories in order to lose weight.

in comparison

> when measured against, when contrasted with

> Mary is very tall **in comparison** to the typical Polynesian woman.

subject to

> able to be affected by; vulnerable to

> His weakness made him **subject to** many diseases.

Vocabulary Exercises

A. Complete the following sentences with words from the list.

install	reduces	involves
retractable	resistance	ratio
indicate	fuel	streamlined

1. Many newer cars have _____ head lamps.

2. Cooking oil is not a good _____.

3. Using brakes _____ the speed of the car.

4. If one person in three cannot read, the _____ of nonreaders to readers is one to three.

5. The new mayor promised to _____ lights on every street in town.

6. The results of the experiment _____ that vitamins are often beneficial.

7. Many bacteria have _____ to penicillin.

8. _____ cars use less fuel.

9. Driving _____ experience.

B. Choose the correct lettered response to complete each numbered statement.

1. Frequent meals help us _____ hunger.
   a. account for
   b. overcome

2. Airplanes are _____ to the forces of gravity and lift.
   a. subject to
   b. in comparison to

3. Those scientists _____ a new use for table salt.
   a. encountered
   b. accounted for

4. _____ French is easier than biochemistry.
   a. To overcome
   b. In comparison,

5. Malnutrition often _____ lower intelligence.
   a. accounts for
   b. is subject to

6. _____ expenses helps you save money.
   a. Cutting down on
   b. Involving

7. A car has the _____ of hundreds of horses.
   a. fuel
   b. force

C. Cross out the word that is wrong.

1. The distance from one side to the other side of the street is its *(length/width)*.

2. We look at the gas gauge *(to reduce/to check)* the amount of fuel.

3. Toys are often *(models/vacuums)* of larger objects.

4. A *(full-size/model)* train can be examined at home.

COMPREHENSION SKILL INDEX
Skimming

Skimming is an important reading skill. Good readers of science often skim the entire selection before reading it carefully, line by line. Skimming is necessary when you want to get a general idea of the following:

1. if the subject is of interest to you
2. if you want to read it at all
3. if you are already familiar with the content of the selection
4. how complex the treatment of the subject is
5. if it presents new findings or if it is a general introduction to the subject
6. if it presents a highly technical or narrow aspect of the subject

How to skim

Open one of your science textbooks. Look at one chapter, but do not read it. Ask yourself the following questions:

1. Does it have more than one paragraph?
2. Does the chapter have one overall title?
3. Are there subheads within the selection?
4. Are there footnotes at the end of the chapter or at the bottom of the pages?
5. Does the author use charts, graphs, illustrations, or formulas?
6. Is a bibliography included?

Skimming

EXERCISES

D. Answer the following questions either in English or in your own language about the chapter *you just skimmed.*

1. What is the general subject of the selection? _____

2. Does the author give the subject full coverage? _____

3. Could the general reader understand this chapter? _____

4. Is the subject a general introduction to the subject as a whole? _____

5. Do you think there is controversy, or disagreement, about the subject? _____

E. Look at the selection on pages 9-11 of the text. Skim it. Do not read it thoroughly. Mark the following statements T if they are true or F if they are false.

_____ 1. The article is about all kinds of moving vehicles.

_____ 2. The article covers the subject of aerodynamics in all its aspects.

_____ 3. The concepts presented are too difficult or sophisticated for the average reader.

_____ 4. You will learn something of value from the selection.

A large fan makes wind for the wind tunnel where clay models and full-size cars are tested.

General Motors

White smoke shows the aerodynamic characteristics of a fuel-efficient car.

General Motors

Reading Selection

Aerodynamics in Car Design

Automobile designers are working on ways to build automobiles that get good gas mileage. One way to do this is to make cars more **streamlined** by **reducing** drag, or wind **resistance**. Scientists define drag as a **force** that retards, or slows, an object that is moving through the air. All moving objects are **subject to** drag. Studies estimate that at 88 kilometers an hour, one-half of the car's **fuel** and more than 60 percent of the car's horsepower are used **to overcome** drag. So if car designers can reduce drag they can improve on the car's gas mileage, or fuel efficiency. **1**

horsepower: a measure of the car's force

efficiency: effective use

To find out more about drag, car designers use engineers who are specialists in aerodynamics. Aerodynamics is a science that **involves** the study of moving air and the forces that act on objects moving through the air. **2**

The aerodynamic specialists measure air resistance in units **indicating** coefficient of drag, or CD. The coefficient of drag is the **ratio** of the amount of wind resistance an object **encounters** to that of a flat plate of the same weight held vertically. As an example of CD, a 1.2- by 2.4-meter piece of plywood held vertically would have a CD of about 1.1. Other shapes would have a lower CD. A watermelon of the same weight as the plywood would have a lower CD. A falling parachute would have a CD of about 1.3. **In comparison,** the typical automobile would have a CD of about 0.45. **3**

plywood: thin wood

Wind Tunnels: The Basic Tool

tool: implement

Engineers use wind tunnels to study the CD of automobiles. Wind tunnels are the basic tool of aerodynamic research. They are used to test design **models,** or smaller representations, of bridges, buildings, spacecraft, and most recently, automobiles. A wind tunnel can have a **width** of 12 to 24 meters and be as long as 275 meters. The tunnel has a special section where a test model is placed.

clay: formable substance

The object tested can be a **full-size** car or a clay model of the real thing. A huge fan blows air into the test section at about 80 kilometers an hour. During this time the aerodynamic specialist **checks** the areas of the car where there may be turbulence, or irregular air movement. Some specialists use powerful lights to check turbulence. Other engineers use smoke, small pieces of paper, or other visible substances in the same way.

4

located: found

trouble: problem

spots: places

rear: back

collects: comes together

The wind tunnel studies have located several trouble spots where drag occurs around the car. One of the major problems is the underside of the car, where there are many exposed parts. This area **accounts for** about 20 percent of the drag. The rear section of the car also presents a problem. All the air that rushes from the front of the car collects in the back and creates a **vacuum,** which pulls the car backwards. Another trouble spot is the area around the window frames. Even license plates, windshields, and side mirrors are areas of drag.

5

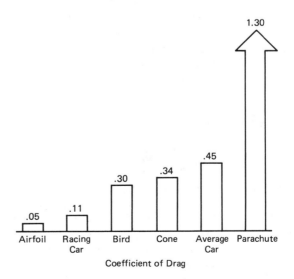

Coefficient of Drag

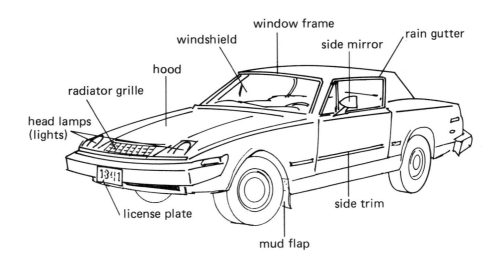

Design Improvements

The wind tunnel studies have helped make many aerodynamic improvements in automobiles. Today many cars have hoods that slope to act as wedges against the wind. Windshields are also better designed to **cut down on** wind resistance. Special dams are **installed** under the front section of the car to reduce the flow, or movement, **6** of air under the car. Other improvements include **retractable** head lamps and smaller radiator grilles. Some designers have stopped using radiator grilles altogether. Others want to eliminate mud flaps, rain gutters, and even side trim to reduce air turbulence.

Aerodynamics will play a major role in the design of future automobiles because of the importance of improving gas mileage. **7** And that means the consumer might see the automobile change drastically in size and shape from what it looks like today.

slope: are placed diagonally

wedges: protectors

dams: collectors

altogether: entirely

mud flaps: mud protectors

eliminate: stop using

gutters: directors

trim: decoration

consumer: buyer

drastically: extremely

COMPREHENSION SKILL INDEX

Comprehension

The most elementary reading comprehension skill is factual recall. In factual recall questions you are asked simply to demonstrate that you understand the facts presented by the author. Often factual recall questions begin with interrogative words, such as *what, who, how, when, why, do, does,* and so on. These questions are also often presented in the form of multiple choice items, true-false questions, matching questions, or as complete-the-following-statement items.

example: Wind tunnels are the basic tool of aerodynamic research.

Sample Factual Recall Questions:

What is the basic tool of aerodynamic research?

Are wind tunnels the basic tool of aerodynamic research?

In what field are wind tunnels the basic tool?

Comprehension

EXERCISE

F. Choose the correct lettered response to complete each numbered statement. Your answers should be based on the reading on pages 9-11.

1. All moving objects _____.
   a. overcome drag
   b. are subject to drag
   c. reduce drag
   d. are streamlined

2. One way to get good gas mileage is _____.
   a. to increase wind resistance
   b. to design automobiles
   c. to reduce drag
   d. to measure air resistance

3. The science that involves the study of moving air is _____.
   a. aerodynamics
   b. air resistance
   c. drag reduction
   d. engineering

4. Aerodynamic specialists measure air resistance _____.
   a. in units indicating CD
   b. vertically
   c. with watermelons
   d. to lower the flat plates

5. Of the following objects, _____ has the lowest CD.
   a. an automobile
   b. 1.2- by 2.4-meter piece of plywood
   c. a falling parachute
   d. a flat plate

6. Engineers study the CD of cars by using _____.
   a. flat plates
   b. bridges
   c. aerodynamic research
   d. wind tunnels

7. Wind tunnels are used to test _____.
   a. spacecraft
   b. bridges
   c. buildings
   d. all of the above

8. There are many exposed parts _____.
   a. in the wind tunnels
   b. on the clay models
   c. on the underside of the car
   d. in the huge fans

9. Well-designed windshields _____.
   a. reduce wind resistance
   b. create a vacuum
   c. cut down on air flow under the car
   d. increase drag

10. Some designers want to eliminate _____.
    a. mud flaps, rain gutters, and air turbulence
    b. head lamps, smaller radiator grilles, and mud flaps
    c. mud flaps, rain gutters, and side trim
    d. wedges, license plates, and side mirrors

COMPREHENSION SKILL INDEX

Confirming Content

It is important to be able to know what the author actually said. The skill of determining what was and was not said is called confirming content. Often you may know that something is true, but you are not sure if the author stated it to be a fact or whether you might have obtained the information from some other source.

example: True or false?

Windshields cause more drag than license plates.

This may be true or not true. The author did not state it, and nothing in the reading would indicate that it is true or not true.

In the next exercise you will be asked to distinguish among true statements, false statements, and statements that cannot be confirmed from what you read.

Confirming Content/Factual Recall

EXERCISE

G. Mark each statement true (T), false (F), or cannot be determined from content (??).

_____ 1. Fuel is used to overcome drag.

_____ 2. A force that slows a moving object is drag.

_____ 3. CD can be measured in a wind tunnel.

_____ 4. All watermelons have lower CDs than plywood.

_____ 5. Parachutes and cars have similar CDs.

_____ 6. In a wind tunnel the light bends at areas where the air flow is irregular.

_____ 7. License plates cause more drag than windshields.

_____ 8. The wind tunnel studies have been the most important source of aerodynamic improvements.

COMPREHENSION SKILL INDEX

Vocabulary in Context

When you read a scientific or technical text in English, you will probably encounter many words you do not know. Searching for them in a bilingual dictionary is time consuming and tiring. Sometimes the procedure takes so long that you become discouraged and close the book.

It is impossible to avoid some dictionary work in foreign language reading. But it is possible to reduce the time you spend using the dictionary by guessing the meaning of unfamiliar words.

The word _or_ is often used to introduce a definition of a word or a phrase, particularly if the author suspects that it may be a new word for the reader. Since science writing so often deals with new ideas, new words often appear within texts. It is important to look for the signal _or_ and to use the definition which it introduces to help you understand the meaning of an unknown word.

example: Lipids, or fats, can be measured in the laboratory.

Models, or smaller representations of full-size objects, are placed in the wind tunnels.

EXERCISE

H. Copy from the reading selection the definition of the following words.

1. drag _____

2. slows _____ _____

3. models _____

4. turbulence _____

5. flow _____

COMPREHENSION SKILL INDEX

Verb Tenses: Present, Present Perfect, Present Progressive

Reminder:

The simple present tense is used for actions that occur now and that generally occur. It is used to state general truths. In science writing this tense is used often because of the frequent use of definitions and rules.

examples: Engineers use wind tunnels to study the CD of automobiles.

At 88 kilometers an hour, more than 60 percent of the car's horsepower is used to overcome drag.

The present perfect tense is used to indicate actions that began in the past and are still occurring.

example: She has used that car since she bought it, even though it gets bad gas mileage.

Sometimes the present perfect tense is used to indicate that something occurred in the very recent past.

example: The wind tunnel studies have located several trouble spots.

This tense is common in science writing, where recent results of experiments are often reported.

The present progressive tense is used to indicate that something is occurring right now and to suggest that it probably did not occur in the past.

example: Wind tunnels are having an effect on car design.

Note that the rules and examples above only cover some of the uses of these tenses. Others will be presented later.

Present, Present Perfect, Present Progressive

EXERCISE

I. Choose the correct lettered response to explain each numbered statement.

1. All moving objects are subject to drag.
   a. This is a general statement of fact.
   b. Moving objects were probably not subject to drag in the past.

2. The wind tunnel studies have located several trouble spots.
   a. This probably happened a long time ago.
   b. This happened in the past, and probably more trouble spots will be found.

3. The studies have helped scientists design better cars.
   a. The studies helped them one time only.
   b. The studies are helping them now but probably did not help them until recently.

4. Air is rushing from the front of the car and is collecting in the rear of the car.
   a. This is a general statement of fact.
   b. This is happening right now.

5. Some engineers have used special lights in the wind tunnel studies.
   a. They don't use them any more.
   b. They are probably still using them now.

COMPREHENSION SKILL INDEX

Simple Noun Compounds

Often two or more nouns are used together so that one of them defines or limits the meaning of the other.

examples: vocabulary list

grammar book

fruit juice

car designer

wind tunnel research

These noun compounds may be confusing unless you are already familiar with them as units. In understanding noun compounds you haven't seen before, it is helpful to remember that the last word in the pair or group is usually the most important. The words that come before it usually are modifiers.

When you reach a confusing pair or group of nouns, it is helpful to ask the question, "What kind of _____?" and try the last noun in the blank space.

Noun Compounds

EXERCISES

J. The reading on pages 9-11 contains twenty-seven different two-word compounds and one three-word compound. The first three are given. Complete the list.

1. gas mileage   10. _____   19. _____

2. wind resistance   11. _____   20. _____

3. car designers   12. _____   21. _____

4. _____   13. _____   22. _____

5. _____   14. _____   23. _____

6. _____   15. _____   24. _____

7. _____   16. _____   25. _____

8. _____   17. _____   26. _____

9. _____   18. _____   27. _____

K. Follow the model.

model: gas mileage ⟶

         What kind of mileage? *gas mileage*

1. gas mileage _____

2. wind resistance _____

3. car designers _____

4. rear section _____

5. license plates _____

6. air turbulence _____

7. trouble spots _____

COMPREHENSION SKILL INDEX   **Figurative Conditional**

Reminder:

     Ordinarily the construction *would* + verb implies the result of a condition that is not real or that is contrary to fact.

example: I would buy that car if it got better gas mileage.
           (It does not get good mileage, so I will not buy it.)

In science writing, in addition to the use in the example, this construction is used in a figurative sense. This often occurs when the writer states something that is theoretical, not literal.

example: A falling parachute would have a CD of about 1.3.

Notice that there is nothing unreal or contrary to fact about the example sentence. The author is implying that the statement is somewhat theoretical, but nonetheless true. The same author could have written the following sentence with no real change in meaning:

example: A falling parachute has a CD of about 1.3.

Figurative Conditional

EXERCISE

L. Choose the correct lettered response to explain each numbered statement.

1. The CD of a 1.2- by 2.4-meter piece of plywood would be about 1.1.
   a. It has a CD of about 1.1.
   b. It does not always have a CD of about 1.1.

2. Cars would get better gas mileage if aerodynamic specialists designed them.
   a. Aerodynamic specialists design cars.
   b. Aerodynamic specialists do not design cars.

3. The typical automobile would have four tires.
   a. The typical automobile has four tires.
   b. The typical automobile has four tires only in certain circumstances.

4. If wind tunnels were big enough, they would be used to test full-size bridges.
   a. Wind tunnels are big enough to test full-size bridges.
   b. Wind tunnels are not big enough to test full-size bridges.

5. Turbulence would be an example of irregular air flow.
   a. Turbulence is not an example of irregular air flow.
   b. Turbulence is an example of irregular air flow.

6. Two and two would equal four.
   a. Two and two equal four.
   b. Two and two would equal four in certain circumstances.

Lasers, Superlight

A laser cutting through metal parts of aircraft brakes

Subtechnical Vocabulary

coronary (adjective)

      relating to the heart

      The **coronary** care department in this hospital has very good equipment.

deep-sea (adjective)

      found in the deep water of the ocean

      Sharks are **deep-sea** animals.

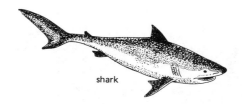

shark

fatty (adjective)

      related to fat; greasy

      When you want to lose weight, it is not good to eat **fatty** foods.

delicate (adjective)

      requiring great care; fragile

      Surgery requires **delicate** finger movements.

artery (noun)

      a blood vessel that takes blood from the heart

      The coronary **arteries** are the arteries closest to the heart.

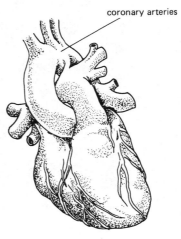

coronary arteries

heart

inner (adjective)

> interior; inside

> The **inner** part of the ear is very delicate.

beam (noun)

> a ray of light

> They saw the airplane in a **beam** of light.

beam of light

clot (noun)

> a thick or solid piece of material that is ordinarily liquid, such as a blood clot

> A blood **clot** in an artery can be dangerous.

count (noun)

> measurement, analysis, rate, index

> Her blood **count** shows that she needs iron.

deposit (noun)

> a material in excess of what the body needs that remains in a body part, such as calcium deposits

> Many athletes have knee problems because of calcium **deposits**.

tube (noun)

a hollow cylindrical vessel that acts as a transport or a passage

A straw is a **tube** used for drinking.

fiber glass (noun)

a material made of a combination of glass fibers and resin

The body of this car is not made of metal. It is made of **fiber glass**.

stroke (noun)

a sudden loss of part of the brain's function caused by an interruption in oxygen flow to that part of the brain

A **stroke** often causes problems on one side of the body.

surgery (noun)

entering the patient's body with a knife or other instrument to treat a condition or to get information

Many cancers can be treated with **surgery**.

obstruction (noun)

a condition occurring when a large object tries to pass through a space that is too small for it

Kidney stones can cause an **obstruction** in the tube that transports the urine.

signs (noun)

symptoms, evidence of

Bleeding and pain are **signs** of ulcers.

to shine (verb)

to give light

The moon **shines** at night.

to emit (verb)

>   to produce

>   X-ray machines **emit** radiation.

to remove (verb)

>   to take off, to take away

>   Surgery is often necessary **to remove** tumors.

to insert (verb)

>   to put in

>   The mother **inserts** the thermometer into the child's mouth.

to detach (verb)

>   to separate

>   The two ends of the belt are not closed; they **are detached**.

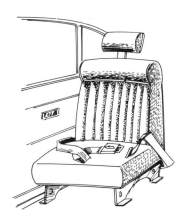

to supply (verb)

> to give; to provide or produce what is necessary
>
> The forests **supply** the world with wood.

Vocabulary of Ideas

to result from [something] (phrasal verb)

> to occur because of [something]
>
> Increased drag can **result from** poor aerodynamic design.

to suffer from [a disease or a condition] (phrasal verb)

> to get, to have [a disease or a condition]
>
> He **suffers from** frequent colds.

to build up (phrasal verb)

> to collect
>
> Problems **build up** and get bigger.

to shut off (phrasal verb)

> to stop
>
> The water **was shut off** by the city.

Vocabulary Exercises

A. Complete the following sentences with words from the list.

strokes	remove	count
supply	beams	suffered from
build up	inserted	clot
sign	emits	shines

1. It is difficult to see when a light _____ in your eyes.

2. We sweep the floor to _____ dirt and dust.

3. _____ are unusual in young people.

4. A _____ can cause the obstruction of an artery or a vein.

5. A poor blood count is often a _____ of disease.

6. A car's head lamps emit two _____ of light.

7. The lungs _____ oxygen to the blood.

8. A fatty deposit can _____ on the inner walls of the arteries.

9. During the surgery the doctor _____ a tube in the patient's throat.

10. My father _____ terrible headaches.

B. Choose the correct lettered response to complete each numbered statement.

1. Heart attacks can _____ an obstruction in a coronary artery.
   a. supply
   b. result from

2. A clot in an artery _____ the blood flow to the heart.
   a. shuts off
   b. builds up

3. When two parts that are normally together are separated, they are _____.
   a. detached
   b. emitted

4. A model car is tested in the _____ section of a wind tunnel.
   a. delicate
   b. inner

5. _____ substances are usually lighter than water.
   a. Fatty
   b. Deep-sea

6. _____ is a material that has many uses.
   a. Fiber glass
   b. Surgery

7. Part of a physical examination is a blood _____.
   a. clot
   b. count

8. _____ can correct some physical problems.
   a. Surgery
   b. Artery

C. Complete each statement with a word from the list at the beginning of the lesson.

1. An _____ carries blood.

2. _____ animals live in the world's oceans.

3. A _____ is something that remains somewhere in the body.

4. A lamp _____ light.

5. A _____ can carry liquid from one place to another.

6. A piece of solidified blood is a _____.

7. Something that is _____ requires care.

8. _____ disease is the same as heart disease.

9. A clot can cause an _____.

COMPREHENSION SKILL INDEX | **Skimming**

Skimming is often necessary when you have very limited time and need to get an idea of what a selection is about. One way to do this is to examine probable topic sentences.

Paragraphs and topic sentences

English paragraphs usually contain information about one aspect of the subject of the whole selection. Often, but not always, the first sentence in the paragraph is a clue to the content of that paragraph.

A sentence that acts as a clue to the content or topic of the paragraph is a "topic sentence."

Skimming for Probable Topic Sentences

EXERCISES

D. Look at the reading on pages 28-29 of this text. Do not read it. Copy the first sentence of each of the nine paragraphs.

1. _____

_____

2. _____

_____

3. _____

_____

4. _____

_____

5. _____

_____

6. _____

_____

7. _____

_____

8. _____

_____

9. _____

_____

E. Look at the nine sentences in Exercise A. Mark the following statements T if they are true or F if they are false.

_____ 1. Lasers are related to light.

_____ 2. Lasers are now used in heart surgery.

_____ 3. There is only one really important use of lasers.

_____ 4. The selection is about present and future uses of lasers.

_____ 5. The author is against the use of lasers.

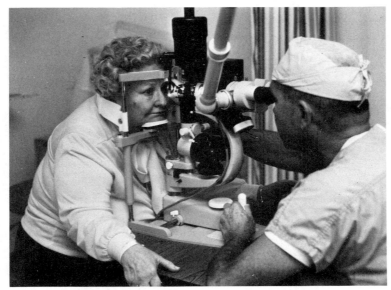

Laser retina reattachment is performed painlessly and without anesthesia.

Russ Kinne, Photo Researchers, Inc.

Reading Selection

super: extraordinarily strong or big

Lasers, Superlight

Today scientists use lasers both in **surgery** and to cut down on unnecessary surgery. A laser is a very strong **beam** of light that is very different from ordinary light.

1

Medical Uses

Doctors use lasers in some eye operations. They use them when operating on a patient who has a **detached** retina. The retina is the **inner** back part of the eye, the part that senses light. Light from an object must strike the retina for seeing to occur.

2

strike: reach, touch

In the past a detached retina caused blindness in that eye. Now the laser makes **delicate** eye surgery possible, and a detached retina no longer means the loss of sight. By carefully directing this super light beam, the doctor can weld the retina to the rest of the eye again. The welding of the retina takes less than a thousandth of a second and is done without anesthesia. Anesthetizing the patient is not necessary, since the patient feels no pain.

3

are interested in using:
want to use

prone: have a high
possibility of having

cholesterol: fatty
material

all it will take: all that
will be necessary

calls for: suggests,
requires

bursts: emissions

feel: think

promise: possibility of
success

established: well
known, common

birthmarks: spots on
the skin; moles

crystal: a structure,
such as quartz or
topaz, having a
characteristic form

straight: not bent

depths: the deepest
parts

currents: water flows

mends: fixes

joins: puts together

Doctors are also interested in using lasers as a surgical tool in operations on people who are prone to heart attacks. In the United States and Canada alone, more than 1.5 million people **suffer from** heart attacks each year. Most of these attacks **result from** an **obstruction** of blood flow through the **coronary arteries.** The coronary arteries **supply** the largest part of the blood to the heart. It is common for people who show **signs** of heart disease to have a high blood cholesterol **count.** The more cholesterol in the blood, the greater the possibility of its **building up** on the inner walls of the arteries as **fatty deposits** called plaques. As the plaques grow, the opening of the artery gets smaller and cuts down on blood flow. If the buildup continues, all it will take is a small **clot** in the bloodstream **to shut off** the circulation and cause a heart attack or a **stroke.**   4

Some heart surgeons are planning to use lasers to vaporize completely the fatty deposits. One plan calls for **inserting** a special **fiber glass tube** into the coronary artery. The end of the tube would be placed near the fatty deposits. Short bursts of laser light **emitted** into the fiber glass tube would destroy the fatty deposits.   5

More studies are needed, but some surgeons feel this plan has promise for some heart patients. At present, though, lasers have many established uses in hospitals; they are used in sterilizing instruments, stopping bleeding, and **removing** birthmarks.   6

What is a Laser?

The laser beam is made up of the same kind of light that **shines** from a lamp. The light from the lamp diffuses, or spreads out, over a room. Simply stated, scientists found that by shining light through certain crystals or gases, they could stop the light from spreading. At the same time the light becomes amplified, or stronger, as mirrors reflect it back and forth through the crystal or gas. In this way the light can move only in one straight beam.   7

Other Uses of Lasers

Lasers have other uses, too. They can light up ocean depths. Ordinarily light illuminates a few meters of deep water. Using a laser beam, however, can light up several hundred meters of water. The superlight will help scientists study **deep-sea** animals and ocean currents. Engineers can use the straight beams to guide their tunnel machines when cutting through rock. The superheat of the laser beam mends and joins pieces of metal and burns away the dirt from stone buildings.   8

We can be certain that in the future there will be more uses for lasers.   9

A laser beam can cut a piece of cast iron.

Photon Sources, Inc.

Comprehension

EXERCISE

F. Choose the correct lettered response to complete each numbered statement.

1. Doctors already use lasers in _____.
   a. eye surgery
   b. heart surgery
   c. reducing fatty deposits
   d. both eye and heart surgery

2. A detached retina _____.
   a. always causes blindness
   b. can be treated
   c. is a super light beam
   d. takes less than a thousandth of a second

3. A laser is _____.
   a. a very strong beam of light
   b. a blade for shaving
   c. an eye operation
   d. the inner back part of the eye

4. Lasers are used _____.
   a. in separating the retina from the eye
   b. in sensing light
   c. by causing seeing to occur
   d. in eye operations

5. In the past _____.
   a. a detached retina always caused blindness
   b. retinas did not detach
   c. blindness caused a detached retina
   d. a detached retina often caused a loss of sight

6. The doctor can weld the retina to the eye again _____.
   a. by directing the laser carefully
   b. by detaching the retina
   c. by welding the retina to the eye
   d. by taking less than a thousandth of a second

7. Because the patient feels no pain, _____.
   a. welding takes very little time
   b. sterilizing the laser is not important
   c. anesthesia is not necessary
   d. bleeding does not occur

8. Shining light through certain crystals and gases _____.
   a. prevents the light from shining
   b. amplifies the light
   c. changes the light to a liquid
   d. detaches the light from its source

Confirming Content

EXERCISE

G. Eight of the following statements say exactly what the author said or say the same thing in another way. Mark those statements with an A. The other seven statements were not made by the author in any way, either directly or indirectly. Mark those statements with a B.

Reminder: Some B statements may be true. Refer to the reading selection, if necessary.

_____ 1. Today eye surgery is usually performed with lasers.

_____ 2. Most heart attacks result from an obstruction in the arteries near the heart.

_____ 3. Cholesterol can leave fatty deposits in the arteries.

_____ 4. Plaques are fatty deposits that come from cholesterol.

_____ 5. Anesthesia is generally necessary in surgery.

_____ 6. In the past, blindness was always caused by detached retinas.

_____ 7. After the retina is welded to the eye, it will not detach again.

_____ 8. Most blood reaches the heart through the coronary arteries.

_____ 9. Plaque causes heart attacks and strokes.

_____ 10. Arteries are tubes.

11. Doctors plan to use lasers to reduce plaques from the artery walls.

_____ 12. Lasers will soon be used for the first time in hospitals.

_____ 13. Laser light is made up of the same kind of light that comes from a lamp.

_____ 14. Lasers are straight beams.

_____ 15. Lasers can light up bigger areas of the ocean depths than ordinary light.

COMPREHENSION SKILL INDEX

Vocabulary in Context

You have already seen that the word *or* is a context clue. Writers often use the word *or* to introduce a synonym or a definition of an unfamiliar word.

The word *called* is often used for a similar reason. This word is frequently used to announce a word which has already been defined.

examples: The obstruction of the coronary artery by a blood clot is called coronary thrombosis.
Superlight beams, called lasers, have many medical uses.

From these examples, it is easy to see why going to the dictionary is often unnecessary. The meaning of the sentence is perfectly clear, even if you do not know the exact translation of *lasers* or *coronary thrombosis*.

At other times an author will simply define a new word for you right in the text itself. When this is done, it is not important to know the translation of the word.

example: In photosynthesis the chloroplasts in plants change dioxide and water into carbohydrates.

Often simply understanding the general meaning of a passage will help you to understand the meaning of a specific word. The following exercise will help you build the skill of understanding vocabulary from context.

Vocabulary in Context

EXERCISE

H. Match the definitions in column B with the terms in column A. Use the reading on pages 28-29 to find the meaning of the words you do not know.

a	*b*
1. to amplify	spreads out
2. means (paragraph 3)	fatty deposits in the artery
3. retina	part of the eye
4. to weld	loss of sight
5. blindness	causes
6. anesthesia	substance that prevents pain
7. plaques	to put separate parts together
8. vaporize	destroy
9. diffuses	to make stronger

Gerunds

Gerunds are very common in scientific and technical writing. Gerunds are nouns that come from adding *-ing* to a verb.

examples:

eat + ing	eating
study + ing	studying
mix + ing	mixing
shine + ing	shining

Gerunds function in the same way as nouns: as subjects and objects.

examples: subject: *Eating* is necessary for good health.

objects: You learn chemistry both by *studying* and *experimenting.*

object: They finished *eating.*

Remember that all verbs can be made into gerunds, but that not all verbs ending in *-ing* are gerunds.

examples: The woman is *teaching* chemistry at the university. (progressive form of verb)

The technician is *reading* and *interpreting* the computer printout. (progressive form of verb)

Running water is often cleaner than *standing* water. (participle, used as modifier)

Gerunds

EXERCISES

I. Fill in the words missing from the two columns.

Verb	*Gerund*
1. prevent	_____
2. _____	dissolving
3. _____	burning
4. shine	_____
5. operate	_____
6. _____	spreading

7. join   _____

8. detach   _____

9. _____   anesthetizing

10. _____   showing

J. Complete the following sentences with a gerund formed from the indicated verb.

1. _____ is important when you are in school. (to study)

2. The function of the eye is _____. (to see)

3. _____ the instruments is the first step in an operation. (to sterilize)

4. You can see small organisms by _____ a microscope. (to use)

5. She liked Dr. Smith's _____. (to teach)

6. We finish _____ arithmetic in the fourth year of school. (to learn)

7. Heat can produce _____. (to burn)

8. _____ is a bad habit. (to smoke)

9. Chlorine is an important chemical in _____ water. (to purify)

10. Water can prevent a fire from _____. (to spread)

K. The reading on pages 28-29 contains fourteen gerunds. Find them and write them in column a.

	a		*b*
1.	_____		_____
2.	_____		_____
3.	_____		_____
4.	_____		_____
5.	_____		_____
6.	_____		_____
7.	_____		_____

8. _____   _____

9. _____   _____

10. _____   _____

11. _____   _____

12. _____   _____

13. _____   _____

14. _____   _____

L. For each gerund in column a, write the verb it comes from in column b.

    example: reading   to read

LESSON THREE

Predicting Earthquakes

California's San Andreas fault can be seen running through the center of the photo.

Subtechnical Vocabulary

to forecast (verb)

> to foresee, to know about and tell about in advance

> Meteorologists study and **forecast** the weather.

to record (verb)

> to write about or keep information in a permanent form

> A graph can be used **to record** the changes in temperature from day to day.

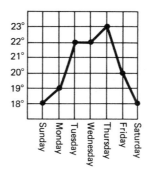

to devise (verb)

> to invent something unusual or something of great originality

> The professor **devised** a new way to correct exams in half the time it usually takes.

to monitor (verb)

> to watch carefully in order to measure changes

> It is important **to monitor** the barometric pressure in order to forecast the weather.

to report (verb)

> to tell about an event; to say that something has happened

> Researchers **report** the results of their experiments at scientific conventions.

to speculate (verb)

to make an educated guess; to form opinions about what will happen in the future

Geologists **speculate** that by the year 2000, accurate earthquake prediction will be common.

earthquake (noun)

a sudden movement of the earth caused by internal forces

Certain areas of the earth get many **earthquakes**.

scale (noun)

a progressive system of measuring units for determining and recording differences in degree; a reference standard used as a system of measurement

Mohs hardness **scale** indicates the relative hardness of rocks in increments of 1 to 10.

damage (noun)

harm or injury

Storms can cause great **damage** to buildings.

damage

reading (noun)

measurement

Diamonds have a **reading** of 10 on Mohs hardness scale.

network (noun)

a connected system of similar things working together

A **network** of scientists all over the world is working on a cure for cancer.

surface (noun)

the exterior of an object or body

The **surface** of calm water is like a mirror.

decay (noun)

degeneration; disintegration

The **decay** of organic substances is necessary for the formation of petroleum.

ground (noun)

the soil on the surface of the earth

In some areas of the northern hemisphere, the **ground** freezes in winter.

level (noun)

relative measurement, density, or position on a scale

There is a high **level** of sodium in the drinking water of certain cities.

stress (noun)

tension or force that, when applied, is capable of deforming objects

Extreme **stress** can bend steel.

slight (adjective)

small, light, not severe

A **slight** change in temperature is difficult to feel with your hand.

Vocabulary of Ideas

over (adverb)

more than

There are **over** five hundred kinds of insects living in this village.

to develop (verb)

to make usable; to invent; to make available

Better computers **are developed** almost every day.

to precede (verb)

to come first, or before something else

A sore throat often **precedes** a cold.

to associate (verb)

to connect; to link in a figurative sense

Infection is a problem often **associated** with burns.

to set up (phrasal verb)

    to create, to implement

    We **set up** a panel of experts to decide which projects were most important.

to come from (phrasal verb)

    to be created by; to result from

    Scurvy is a disease that **comes from** a deficiency of vitamin C.

Vocabulary Exercises

A. Choose the lettered response that is most similar to the italicized word.

1. It is important to *watch* the radiation levels in areas where radioactive materials are kept.
   a. monitor
   b. forecast
   c. report

2. If too much *tension* is applied to an object, it may break.
   a. damage
   b. earthquake
   c. stress

3. We *implemented* a new procedure to make university registration easier.
   a. set up
   b. reported
   c. monitored

4. Scientists have *said* that many bacteria are now resistant to penicillin.
   a. recorded
   b. speculated
   c. reported

5. Newton understood the force of gravity when he saw an apple fall to the *earth*.
   a. surface
   b. ground
   c. scale

6. Earthquakes can cause much *harm* in a very short time.
   a. damage
   b. decay
   c. stress

B. Unscramble the word in parentheses to complete the following sentences.

1. There is a _____ difference between the words *forecast* and *predict*. (GLITSH)

2. Many people would like to _____ a way to learn languages more easily. (SIVEED)

3. Seismic ocean waves are often _____ with earthquakes. (COSTADISAE)

4. Often small earthquakes, or tremors, _____ larger ones. (CREEPED)

5. Certain minerals emit a high _____ of radioactivity. (VEELD)

6. Many theoreticians _____ about the future of lasers. (PELUSTECA)

7. Death and _____ are two associated processes. (CYADE)

8. The arteries and veins are a _____ for blood transportation. (KREWTON)

C. Choose the correct lettered response to complete each numbered statement.

1. A blood pressure _____ of more than 140/90 is considered high.
   a. scale
   b. reading

2. An earthquake _____ when the earth suddenly moves.
   a. takes place
   b. precedes

3. On a _____ of one to ten, how effective is aspirin for headache?
   a. surface
   b. scale

4. Oceanographers _____ a change in water pollution levels after the new rules are implemented.
   a. record
   b. forecast

5. Most damage occurs when earthquakes take place near the _____ of the earth, and not deep inside it.
   a. surface
   b. stress

6. Sensitive instruments can _____ slight movement along cracks, or openings, in the earth's surface.
   a. record
   b. come from

7. _____ 20 percent of the earth's inhabitants live in China.
   a. Slight
   b. Over

8. Scientists all over the world are _____ a network of emergency communication media.
   a. associating
   b. developing

9. _____ and storms are dangerous natural events.
   a. Earthquakes
   b. Stresses

Skimming

As you know, you can get a fast, general idea about a reading selection by reading topic sentences. Authors often, but not always, place topic sentences first in each paragraph.

How do you know if a particular sentence is the topic sentence of the paragraph? In the reading on pages 9-11 there are seven paragraphs. Below are the sentences that begin each of the seven paragraphs.

1. Automobile designers are working on ways to build automobiles that get good gas mileage.
2. To find out more about drag, car designers use engineers who are specialists in aerodynamics.
3. The aerodynamic specialists measure air resistance in units indicating coefficient of drag, or CD.
4. Engineers use wind tunnels to study the CD of automobiles.
5. The wind tunnel studies have located several trouble spots where drag occurs around the car.
6. The wind tunnel studies have helped make many aerodynamic improvements in automobiles.
7. Aerodynamics will play a major role in the design of future automobiles.

All these sentences are topic sentences. Each announces to the reader what the entire paragraph will be about. If you look at the other sentences contained in the paragraphs, you will find that they present details or other information that support the topic sentence.

In skimming the first sentence of each paragraph in a new reading, it is important for the reader to know whether that sentence is or is not a topic sentence. If it is not, it is necessary to find another sentence that is.

When the first sentence of the paragraph is not the topic sentence, there is a good chance that the topic sentence will be either the second or the last sentence in the paragraph.

The following exercise will help illustrate the difference between topic sentences and other sentences.

Skimming

EXERCISE

D. The following sentences are taken from the reading on pages 28-29. Some of them are topic sentences. Mark them T. The other sentences give important factual details but are not topic sentences. Mark them D.

_____ 1. Doctors use lasers in some eye operations.

_____ 2. The retina is the inner back part of the eye, the part that senses light.

_____ 3. The welding of the retina takes less than a thousandth of a second and is done without anesthesia.

_____ 4. Doctors are also interested in using lasers as a surgical tool in operations on people who are prone to heart attacks.

_____ 5. Most of these attacks result from an obstruction of blood flow through the coronary artery.

_____ 6. One plan calls for inserting a special fiber glass tube into the coronary artery.

_____ 7. They can light up ocean depths.

_____ 8. Lasers have other uses, too.

A scientist installs portable seismic recording equipment in the ground near Mount St. Helens, where hundreds of earthquakes occurred in 1980.

U.S. Geological Survey, Department of the Interior

A woman searches for relatives in a building damaged by a strong earthquake in the city of Laoag, the Philippines in 1983.

UPI Photo

Reading Selection

Predicting Earthquakes

Can **earthquakes** be predicted? Scientists are working on programs to predict where and when an earthquake will occur. They hope **to develop** an early warning system that can be used **to forecast** earthquakes so that lives can be saved. The scientists who are involved in this work are called seismologists. The word *seismologist* comes from the Greek word *seismos*, meaning earthquake.

deadly: capable of causing death

Earthquakes are the most dangerous and deadly of all natural events. They occur in many parts of the world. Giant earthquakes have been **recorded** in Iran, China, Guatemala, Chile, India, and Alaska. Two of the biggest earthquakes that were ever recorded took place in China and Alaska. These earthquakes measured about 8.5 on the Richter **Scale**. The Richter Scale was **devised** by Charles Richter in 1935, and compares the energy level of earthquakes. An earthquake that measures a 2 on the scale can be felt but causes little **damage**. One that measures 4.5 on the scale can cause **slight** damage, and an earthquake that has a **reading** of **over** 7 can cause major damage. It is important to note that a reading of 4 indicates

energy: force

1

2

a quake ten times as strong as one with a reading of 3. Seismologists want to be able to predict those earthquakes that have a reading of over 4 on the Richter Scale.

How do earthquakes occur? Earthquakes are caused by the shifting of rocks along cracks, or faults, in the earth's crust. The fault is produced when rocks near each other are pulled in different directions. The best-known fault in North America is the San Andreas fault in the state of California in the United States.   **3**

The nations that are actively involved in earthquake prediction programs include Japan, China, the Soviet Union, and the United States. These countries have **set up** seismic **networks** in areas of their countries where earthquakes are known to occur. These networks are on the alert for warning signs that show the weakening of rock layers that can **precede** an earthquake. Many kinds of seismic instruments are used by the networks to **monitor** the movements of the earth's crust. One of the instruments is a seismograph. It can detect vibrations in rock layers thousands of kilometers away. Tiltmeters are used to record **surface** tilt along fault lines. Seismologists use gravimeters to measure and record changes in local gravity. The scientists also check water in deep wells. They watch for changes in the water **level** and temperature that **are associated** with movement along faults.   **4**

Seismologists in China, the Soviet Union, and the United States measure radon in **ground** water. Radon is a gas that **comes from** the radioactive **decay** of radium in rocks. The gas flows through the ground and dissolves in underground streams and wells. Scientists **speculate** that the amount of radon increases in the ground when rocks layers shift, exposing new rock, and thus more radon. Chinese and Soviet seismologists **have reported** that in places where **stress** is building up, the radon levels in the water build up too. When the radon levels of the water subside and drop back to normal readings, an earthquake may occur. United States scientists have also placed radon monitoring stations in earthquake zones, particularly California. However, all the scientists agree that more data is necessary to prove that radon levels in water are associated with the possible birth of an earthquake.   **5**

Earthquake prediction is in its infancy. Everyone agrees that earthquakes cannot be predicted with any reliability. Scientists have only a partial understanding of the physical processes that cause earthquakes. Much more research has to be done. New and more up-to-date methods have to be found for collecting earthquake data and analyzing it. However, seismologists have had some success in predicting earthquakes. Several small earthquakes were predicted in New York State, in the eastern part of the United States. Chinese seismologists predicted a major one in Haicheng in 1975, and Soviet scientists predicted a major one in Garm in 1978. While this is a small start, it is still a beginning.   **6**

More than 3000 people were killed and 200,000 were left homeless in a 1980 earthquake in Lioni, Italy.

UPI Photo

Comprehension

EXERCISE

E. Mark the following statements T if they are true or F if they are false.

_____ 1. Scientists are interested in both when and where an earthquake will occur.

_____ 2. There are some natural events that are more deadly and dangerous than earthquakes.

_____ 3. Chile has never had a really bad earthquake.

_____ 4. The Richter Scale helps scientists locate strong earthquakes.

_____ 5. The higher the number on the Richter Scale, the greater the energy level of the earthquake.

_____ 6. Seismologists want to be able to predict strong earthquakes.

_____ 7. There is an important fault in the state of California.

_____ 8. Japan, China, the Soviet Union, and the United States have set up seismic networks in all parts of their countries.

_____ 9. The weakening of rock layers is one warning sign that an earthquake might occur.

_____ 10. A seismograph records tilt, or inclination of rock layers away from the horizontal.

_____ 11. Gravimeters, tiltmeters, and seismographs are all used in earthquake prediction.

_____ 12. The water level in wells is somehow connected to movement along fault lines.

_____ 13. Scientists also monitor temperature changes in well water when they are looking for earthquake warning signs.

_____ 14. Chinese and Soviet seismologists are not interested in measuring radon levels in well water.

_____ 15. It has now been proved that radon levels in water are associated with the birth of an earthquake.

_____ 16. Earthquakes can be accurately predicted.

_____ 17. More study in this area is needed.

COMPREHENSION SKILL INDEX

Vocabulary in Context

Remember that it is often possible to understand the meaning of a new word from the text that surrounds it. When this is possible, it is not necessary to go to the dictionary.

example: They hope to develop an early warning system that can be used to predict earthquakes.

The example sentence tells you what an early warning system is. If you find some reason why it is necessary to translate _early_ or _warning_ into your own language, you may choose to go to the dictionary. Note, however, that even without a literal translation of these words, you are able to understand what an early warning system is.

Vocabulary in Context

EXERCISE

F. Choose the correct lettered response to complete each numbered statement. The paragraph in which the word appeared is given to help you answer.

1. Predictions (title and ¶ 1) _____.
   a. indicate when something will take place
   b. report occurrences of earthquakes

2. An early warning system (¶ 1) _____.
   a. predicts earthquakes
   b. is not modern

3. Seismologists (¶ 1) _____.
   a. study the size of natural events
   b. are scientists who are involved in the study of earthquakes

4. Cracks (¶ 3) are _____.
   a. faults
   b. long, shifting movements

5. Seismic instruments (¶ 4) _____.
   a. watch for changes in the location of areas of the earth's crust
   b. monitor sounds made by the earth's movement

6. A seismograph (¶ 4) _____.
   a. feels faraway vibrations
   b. is a special paper used by seismologists

7. When something subsides (¶ 5), it probably _____.
   a. decreases
   b. increases

8. "Partial" (¶ 6) means _____.
   a. "complete"
   b. "incomplete"

*Seismograph shows a reading of an earthquake measuring 5.5 on
the Richter Scale.*

U.S. Geological Survey, Department of the Interior

Passive Voice

Scientific and technical writing is full of sentences written in the passive voice. Many intermediate-level readers have difficulty understanding these sentences. Contrast and review the formation and meaning of active and passive sentences. The following example sentences illustrate active and passive voice.

examples: *active voice:*   any verb; subject is performer of verb's action

     subject   verb

Earthquakes often cause great damage.

    subject   verb

Geologists will hold a meeting in Toronto next week.

    subject   verb

The graph recorded the baby's weight gain during a two-month period.

        subject   verb

The ethics commission has monitored organ transplant operations since these became common.

          passive voice: form of *be* combined with the past participle of another verb; subject is receiver of verb's action

    subject   verb

Great damage is often caused by earthquakes.

        subject   verb

Next week in Toronto a meeting will be held by geologists.

      subject   verb

The baby's weight gain during a two-month period was recorded on the graph.

               subject   verb

Since these became common, organ transplant operations have been monitored by the ethics commission.

People who write about science and technology choose the passive voice for a variety of reasons:

1. to emphasize a phenomenon or a process, instead of the scientist
2. to make a sentence more impersonal
3. to vary the structure of successive sentences for interest
4. to conform to the style other writers use

Passive Voice

EXERCISE

G. Mark the following sentences A for active voice or P for passive voice.

_____ 1. The principal causes of earthquakes are listed on the chart.

_____ 2. Wind tunnel studies should be performed on all new cars and air-planes.

_____ 3. In the past, eye surgery was not possible without anesthesia.

_____ 4. It is difficult to understand the concept of drag.

_____ 5. Rain falls every afternoon from May to October.

_____ 6. The man was bitten by the dog.

_____ 7. Paper is made from wood.

_____ 8. The factories are working day and night.

_____ 9. Scientists have associated high air pollution levels with temperature inversions.

_____ 10. The world's oceans are full of possibilities for exploration.

_____ 11. Doctors have used lasers in a variety of ways.

_____ 12. She has monitored pollution levels for two years.

COMPREHENSION SKILL INDEX

The Past Participle

The past participles of regular verbs are formed by adding *-ed* or *-d* to the root form of the verb. These are easily recognizable, as long as you know the meaning of the root verb.

examples:	Root Verb	Past Participle
	(to) talk	talked
	(to) smoke	smoked

Some verbs have past participles that are irregularly formed but are easy to recognize. While they may be difficult to master and use, they usually do not cause a comprehension problem.

examples:	Root Verb	Past Participle
	(to) study	studied
	(to) read	read
	(to) come	come

The following eighty-nine verbs are found frequently in scientific and technical writing, and have irregular past participles that are harder to recognize than are the regular ones. You must also be able to recognize and understand these past participles if you want to be a successful reader of scientific and technical English. (Note further that knowing these past participles will also help you understand sentences written in any of the perfect tenses of English written in the active voice.)

Root Verb	Past Participle
arise	arisen
be	been
bear	borne
begin	begun
bend	bent
bind	bound
bite	bitten
bleed	bled
blow	blown
break	broken
breed	bred
bring	brought
build	built
catch	caught
choose	chosen
cling	clung
creep	crept
deal	dealt
dig	dug
do	done
draw	drawn
drink	drunk
drive	driven
eat	eaten
fall	fallen
feed	fed
feel	felt
fight	fought
find	found
fly	flown
forget	forgotten

Root Verb	Past Participle
freeze	frozen
get	gotten
give	given
go	gone
grind	ground
grow	grown
hang	hung
have	had
hear	heard
hide	hidden
hold	held
keep	kept
know	known
lay	laid
lead	led
leave	left
lie	lain
light	lit (or lighted)
lose	lost
make	made
mean	meant
meet	met
prove	proven (or proved)
ride	ridden
ring	rung
rise	risen
say	said
see	seen
seek	sought
send	sent
shake	shaken
shine (to polish)	shined
shine (to light)	shone

Root Verb	Past Participle
shoot	shot
show	shown
shrink	shrunk (or shrunken)
sleep	slept
slide	slid
spin	spun
stand	stood
stick	stuck
sting	stung
strike	stricken
strike	struck
sweep	swept
swell	swollen
swim	swum
take	taken
teach	taught
tear	torn
tell	told
think	thought
throw	thrown
understand	understood
weave	woven
wind	wound
wring	wrung
write	written

The Past Participle

EXERCISE

H. Supply the root verb for the italicized past participle in each of the following sentences.

example: In the past, patients were *bled* to help them eliminate poisonous

substances. ___*bleed*_____

1. When ordinary lights were *shone* in the ocean depths, the divers could see only a few meters. _____

2. The records of the wind tunnel studies were *lost* when the laboratory changed owners. _____

3. The meaning of many past participles is *hidden* by unusual spellings. _____

_____

4. Corn was *ground* in order to make flour. _____

5. This is the second time this course has been *taught* by Mrs. Brown. _____

_____

6. The results of these experiments will be *left* for the students to interpret. _____

_____

7. After the car was *driven* into the wind tunnel, the door of the wind tunnel was closed.

_____

8. A method for predicting earthquakes has been *sought* for many years. _____

_____

9. The surface of the lens was *swept* clean of any dust that might interfere with its clarity. _____

10. Earthquakes are *thought* to play an important role in volcano formation. _____

_____

COMPREHENSION SKILL INDEX   **Passive Voice (continued)**

Remember that the key to understanding sentences in the passive voice is in knowing that the subject is the receiver of the verb's action and in recognizing and understanding the past participle. The following exercises are devised to give you practice in these skills.

Passive Voice (continued)

EXERCISES

I. In the following fifteen sentences taken from the reading, a passive voice verb is italicized. Circle the receiver of that verb's action and draw an arrow from the verb to it. Then choose a or b to indicate that you understand the meaning of the sentence.

example: (Earthquakes) *can be predicted.*

1. They hope to develop an early warning system that *can be used* to forecast earthquakes, so that lives can be saved.
   a. The early warning system will forecast earthquakes.
   b. The earthquakes forecast an early warning system.

2. These scientists *are called* seismologists.
   a. The scientists call the seismologists.
   b. Seismologist is the name used for these scientists.

3. Giant earthquakes *have been recorded* in Iran, China, Guatemala, Chile, India, and Alaska.
   a. There have been giant earthquakes in Iran, China, Guatemala, Chile, India, and Alaska.
   b. Giant earthquakes have recorded Iran, China, Guatemala, Chile, India, and Alaska.

4. The Richter Scale *was devised* by Charles Richter in 1935, and compares the energy levels of earthquakes.
   a. The Richter Scale devised Charles Richter, who was compared to the energy level of earthquakes.
   b. Charles Richter devised the Richter Scale, which compares earthquake energy levels.

5. An earthquake that measures a 2 on the Richter Scale *can be felt* but causes little damage.
   a. Little damage is caused by an earthquake that measures a 2.
   b. An earthquake is caused by little damage that measures a 2.

6. Earthquakes *are caused* by the shifting of rocks along cracks, or faults, in the earth's crust.
   a. The shifting of rocks caused earthquakes.
   b. The cracks cause the shifting of rocks.

7. The fault *is produced* when rocks near each other are pulled in different directions.
   a. Producing the fault pulls the rocks near each other.
   b. Pulling the rocks in different directions produces the fault.

8. Earthquakes *are known* to exist in many parts of the world.
   a. Many parts of the world have known earthquakes.
   b. Many parts of the world are known to exist.

9. Many kinds of seismic instruments *are used* by the networks to monitor the movement of the earth's crust.
   a. The networks use seismic instruments to monitor the movement of the earth's crust.
   b. The movement of the earth's crust uses the networks to monitor many kinds of seismic instruments.

10. Tiltmeters *are used* to record surface tilt along fault lines.
    a. Surface tilt records fault lines.
    b. Surface tilt is recorded by tiltmeters.

One geophysicist studies tremor readings while the other enters data into the computer to try to locate the earthquake.

U.S. Geological Survey, Department of the Interior

11. Changes in the water level and temperature *are associated* with movement along fault lines.
    a. Water level and temperature change with movement along fault lines.
    b. Movement along fault lines associates changes in the water level.

12. Earthquakes *cannot be predicted* with any reliability.
    a. Reliability cannot predict any earthquakes.
    b. It is impossible to predict earthquakes with any reliability.

13. Much more research *has to be done.*
    a. It is necessary to do much more research.
    b. Research has much more to be done.

14. New and more up-to-date methods *have to be found* for collecting earthquake data and analyzing it.
    a. Collecting earthquake data and analyzing it has found new and more up-to-date methods.
    b. It is necessary to find new and more up-to-date earthquake data collection methods.

15. Several small earthquakes *were predicted* in New York State.
    a. Several small earthquakes predicted in New York State.
    b. In New York State several small earthquakes were predicted.

J. Give the root verb for the italicized past participles in the following sentences taken from the reading.

1-2. The scientists who are *involved* in this work are *called* seismologists. _____

3. The Richter Scale was *devised* by Charles Richter in 1935. _____

4. An earthquake that measures a 2 on the Richter Scale can be *felt*. _____

5. These countries have set up seismic networks in areas where earthquakes are *known* to occur. _____

6. They watch for changes in the water level and temperature that are *associated* with movement along faults. _____

7. Much more research has to be *done*. _____

8. New and more up-to-date methods have to be *found*. _____

Noun Compunds

EXERCISES

K. Follow the example. Practice understanding compound nouns.

example: energy levels ⟶
What kind of levels? *Energy levels*

1. earthquake prediction programs _____

2. warning signs _____

3. water level _____

L. Make six two-word compounds by combining the following twelve nouns in pairs. Use each word only once.

warning	ground	earthquake	layers
tilt	surface	level	water
radon	system	rock	zones

1. _____

2. _____

3. _____

4. _____

5. _____

6. _____

Verb Tense Comprehension

EXERCISE

M. Choose the correct lettered response to explain each numbered statement adapted from the reading.

1. Giant earthquakes have been recorded in Iran, China, Guatemala, Chile, India, and Alaska.
   a. They probably took place a long time ago.
   b. These were recorded in the past but probably will occur again.

2. An earthquake that measures 4.5 on the scale causes slight damage.
   a. This is a general statement of fact.
   b. This is happening right now.

3. Tiltmeters are used to record surface tilt along fault lines.
   a. This used to happen in the past.
   b. This is happening at present.

A seismologist testing earthquake prediction instrumentation

U.S. Geological Survey, Department of the Interior

4. Chinese and Soviet seismologists have reported that in places where stress is building up, the radon levels in the water build up too.
   a. They have already reported this, but recently.
   b. They are in the process of reporting the buildup right now.

5. When radon levels subside and drop back to normal readings, an earthquake occurs.
   a. This is a general statement of fact.
   b. This was probably not true in the past.

6. However, seismologist have had some success in predicting earthquakes.
   a. They have had some success but will probably have not more.
   b. They will probably have more success.

LESSON FOUR

Amaranth, a Promising Food Crop

A wheat crop is harvested with a combine.

Subtechnical Vocabulary

crop (noun)

plants grown commercially

The citrus fruit **crop** this year was damaged by extreme cold.

diet (noun)

the everyday or usual food eaten by a person or an animal

A growing child's **diet** should be high in vitamins.

grain (noun)

the seed or fruit of grasses such as rice, wheat, or oats

Grains are one of the most important sources of food throughout the world.

species (noun)

a kind or a variety of living thing; the group of most closely related organisms

There are many **species** of cactus growing in the Atacama desert.

species of cactus

compound (noun)

a chemical combination of two or more different elements

In a **compound** the elements usually cannot be separated.

yield (noun)

the quantity of a crop produced from a specific planting in one season

The **yield** of this year's corn crop is better than last year's.

offspring (noun)

young animals or plants produced from a particular pair of parents

The **offspring** of healthy parents are usually bigger than the offspring of unhealthy parents.

trait (noun)

characteristic

Many **traits** are genetically determined.

pest (noun)

a plant or animal that causes damage to another

The mosquito is a serious **pest** in many parts of the world.

mosquito

environment (noun)

the physical conditions in the area around an organism or a group of organisms

Most tropical plants grow best in a humid **environment**.

hardy (adjective)

strong; difficult to damage

Hardy plants can grow in a variety of environments.

wild (adjective)

> not grown by humans; naturally occurring
>
> Many animals live on a diet of **wild** berries.

hereditary (adjective)

> genetically determined; genetically transmitted
>
> Eye color and hair color are **hereditary** traits.

uniform (adjective)

> the same
>
> It is easier to harvest plants of **uniform** size and maturity.

adaptable (adjective)

> flexible; able to function in a wide range of environments
>
> Humans are **adaptable** to a variety of difficulties.

marginal (adjective)

> on the line between good and bad, between adequate and inadequate
>
> Most plants require a certain environment to grow in, and are not adaptable to **marginal** conditions.

essential (adjective)

> necessary
>
> Protein is an **essential** nutrient for growth and repair of the body.

to cultivate (verb)

> to plant and take care of crops
>
> Potatoes **were cultivated** by the Incas of Peru.

to harvest (verb)

to gather, to pick, or to cut a crop that is fully grown

Corn **is harvested** in September in many places in the northern hemisphere.

to breed (verb)

to cause to produce offspring

Race horses **are bred** for speed and hardiness.

to cross (verb)

to breed an individual of one species with one of another species in order to produce a different or a better offspring

When you **cross** a male donkey with a female horse, a mule results.

mule, horse, donkey.

to mature (verb)

to grow to adulthood

Dogs and cats **mature** in their first year of life.

to extend (verb)

to increase the size or range of something

Reducing heart attacks in individuals prone to heart disease **could extend** their lives several years.

Vocabulary of Ideas

close to (adverbial expression)

almost

There are **close to** one hundred students in this class.

a wide range of (adverbial expression)

>a large variety of

>There is not usually **a wide range of** differences between individual plants in a good crop.

feasibility (noun)

>possibility; probability of success

>What is the **feasibility** of using lasers to reduce arterial plaque?

to miss (verb)

>not to have; to lack

>This car **is missing** several important parts: the side mirrors, the windshield wipers, and the tires.

to come along (phrasal verb)

>to appear

>Insulin was the first medicine **to come along** that prevented diabetics from dying.

to take + time expression (idiomatic expression)

>to require a certain amount of time

>In many countries a complete medical education **takes close to ten years.**

to be short of something (idiomatic expression)

>not to have enough of something

>We **are short of money** for essential research.

Vocabulary Exercises

A. Choose the correct lettered response to complete each numbered statement.

1. Corn and rice are _____.
   a. pests
   b. grains

2. We don't know the economic _____ of cultivating wild strawberries commercially.
   a. feasibility
   b. environment

3. Grains are an essential part of everyone's _____.
   a. diet
   b. crops

4. When a person is fully grown, he or she has _____.
   a. bred
   b. matured

5. Agriculturists are always trying to breed crops that are resistant to _____.
   a. traits
   b. pests

6. A high protein diet is _____ for pregnant women.
   a. marginal
   b. essential

7. When a person doesn't have enough food, he or she is _____ food.
   a. short of
   b. close to

8. The laser beam repair of detached retinas is the first nonsurgical method that has

   _____.
   a. come along
   b. matured

9. Crops are _____.
   a. cultivated
   b. wild

10. Humans are _____ to a wide range of conditions.
    a. adaptable
    b. uniform

11. It _____ several months from the planting of a crop to the harvesting of it.
    a. takes
    b. matures

B. Mark the following statements T if they are true or F if they are false.

_____ 1. Marginal air is probably somewhat polluted.

_____ 2. The farmer first plants the crop and later harvests it.

_____ 3. Salt water is an example of a compound.

_____ 4. The crop's yield is the same as its hardiness.

_____ 5. Pests belong to the same species: *specius pestis*.

_____ 6. It is impossible to cross a dog with a cat.

_____ 7. Offspring do not result from breeding.

_____ 8. Some traits probably come from the environment.

_____ 9. A wide range of friends makes life more interesting.

_____ 10. In 1989 close to 10 percent of this century will be past.

C. Unscramble the cue word in column b to match it with its definition in column a.

a	b
1. not have	HYDRA
2. genetically transmitted	CORP
3. commercially grown plants	LIWD
4. to make larger	PONGSRIFF
5. same	MOVERTENNIN
6. physical conditions	ISMS
7. results of breeding	MUFNOIR
8. strong	NEXTED
9. uncultivated	DEARTHIREY

Corn and wheat are planted together in alternating rows.
USDA Photo

The topic sentence gives you an idea of the kind of information you can expect to find in the paragraph. In the next exercise you will have a chance to see this clearly.

Look at the following eight topic sentences from the reading on pages 69-70. (Note that each of these sentences is the first sentence of one of the eight paragraphs.)

1. Agriculturists believe amaranth is the most promising cereal crop to come along in recent years.
2. It is not a new idea to grow amaranth as a foodstuff.
3. It has been discovered that amaranth is a highly nutritious food.
4. Amaranth can be ground into flour and made into baked goods.
5. It is true that breeding a wild plant into a major food crop such as wheat requires much research time.
6. Plant researchers are now working on developing new hybrids.
7. Some farm experts feel that selling the amaranth grain commercially may not be easy.
8. Amaranth may be the kind of high-protein grain that poorer countries need to feed people who go hungry every day.

Skimming

EXERCISE

D. The following sentences also appear in the same selection. To the left of each sentence, choose the paragraph you would put it in.

Paragraph Number

_____ 1. The hybrid must also be adaptable to a wide range of environmental conditions.

_____ 2. Bread made from amaranth flour is heavy and very compact when compared with the light and airy bread common in North America.

_____ 3. It may be that in countries that are short of an adequate food supply, amaranth is the foodstuff of the future.

_____ 4. Many questions arise about the feasibility of amaranth cultivation.

_____ 5. Some agriculturists believe the plant can be grown commercially in many environments to help feed a hungry world.

_____ 6. However, when Cortés and his Spanish army invaded Mexico, they destroyed the crop completely.

_____ 7. Presently there are several problems in growing amaranth as a crop.

_____ 8. The plant's seed is high in protein, and it contains an important amino acid called lysine.

A scientist studies amaranth harvest yields.
USDA Photo by Fred S. Witte

Reading Selection

Amaranth, a Promising Food Crop

promising: causing optimism

cereal: grain

unfading: permanent

Agriculturists believe amaranth is the most promising cereal **crop to come along** in recent years. Amaranth is a plant whose name comes from a Greek word meaning "unfading." Some agriculturists believe the plant can be grown commercially in many **environments** to help feed a hungry world.   **1**

foodstuff: food source, basic food

It is not a new idea to grow amaranth as a foodstuff. In Mexico during the sixteenth century, the Aztecs **cultivated** it. The plant was an important part of their **diet**. It has been shown that the Aztecs **harvested close to** 6,000 metric tons of the **grain** each year. However, when Cortés and his Spanish army invaded Mexico, they destroyed the crop completely. Today only a few **wild** and unculti- vated **species** of amaranth exist, and it is rarely used as a food in Mexico.   **2**

metric ton: 1,000 kilograms

nutritious: providing substances essential for life

It has been discovered that amaranth is a highly nutritious food. The plant's seed is high in protein, and it contains an impor- tant amino acid called lysine. Amino acids are organic **compounds** that are the building blocks of protein. Lysine is an **essential** amino acid that **is missing** in wheat, rice, and corn. The leaves of some varieties compare in taste and nutritional value with spinach and other vegetable greens.   **3**

greens: leafy vegetables

Amaranth can be ground into flour and made into baked

goods: products

snack: food eaten between regular meals

given: specific

accustomed to: used to

consuming: eating

to support: to grow successfully

goods. Bread made from amaranth flour is heavy and very compact when compared with the light and airy bread common in North America. The flour can also be used for cakes, cookies, and crackers, as well as high-protein breakfast cereals and snack foods. **4**

It is true that **breeding** a wild plant into a major food crop such as wheat requires much research time. Agriculturists know that it has **taken hundreds of years** of breeding different varieties of corn to get the kinds we have today. Presently there are several problems in growing amaranth as a crop. Because it is a wild plant, it is hard to predict the date when the crop will be ready to be harvested. It is also impossible to know the expected height of the individual plants or the **yield** of a given amount of seed. It is important for economic reasons to breed a plant of **uniform** height and one that can be harvested at a specific time each year. **5**

Plant researchers are now working on developing new hybrids. A hybrid is an **offspring** resulting from the **crossing** of parent plants differing in **hereditary traits**. The hybrid is more vigorous, or stronger, than either parent. Researchers want to develop a hybrid that is resistant to disease and insect **pests** and at the same time provides a high yield of grain per hectare. The hybrid must also be **adaptable** to **a wide range of** environmental conditions. A hybrid that **matures** in three months or less would **extend** the possibility of growing amaranth in cold areas with short growing seasons. **6**

Some farm experts feel that selling the amaranth grain commercially may not be easy. Wheat is still the major crop demanded by most countries. Many questions arise about the **feasibility** of amaranth cultivation. How much will it cost to grow and harvest amaranth? Does the crop require special machinery to harvest it? Will a new grain be acceptable to people who are accustomed to consuming other grains? It will be some time before we have answers to all these questions. **7**

Amaranth may be the kind of high-protein grain that poorer countries need to feed people who go hungry every day. Amaranth is a **hardy** plant that grows in **marginal** areas unable to support other crops. It may be that in countries that **are short of** an adequate food supply, amaranth is the foodstuff of the future. **8**

Comprehension

EXERCISE

E. Choose the correct lettered response to answer each of the following questions.

1. What do agriculturists believe?
   a. Amaranth will grow in any environment.
   b. Amaranth is the most promising cereal crop to come along in recent years.
   c. Amaranth can be advertised in many areas.

Barley is an important cereal crop.
USDA Photo

2. What happened to the amaranth that was grown in Mexico?
   a. It was destroyed by the Spaniards.
   b. Cortés sent it to Spain.
   c. It was wild and uncultivated.

3. What do wheat, rice, and corn not have?
   a. the taste and nutritional value of spinach
   b. amino acids
   c. lysine

4. What can be done with amaranth?
   a. It can be ground into wheat, rice, and corn.
   b. It can be used to make bread.
   c. It can be combined with spinach and other vegetable greens.

5. What is generally true about breeding wild plants into food crops?
   a. It is ready to be harvested.
   b. It is developing new hybrids.
   c. It takes a long time.

Confirming Content

EXERCISE

F. Some of the following statements say exactly what the author said or say the same thing in another way. Mark those statements with an A. The other statements were not made by the author in any way, either directly or indirectly. Mark those statements with a B.

Reminder: Some B statements may be true.

_____ 1. Amaranth is more nutritious than wheat, rice, and corn.

_____ 2. The Aztecs produced a large amaranth crop each year.

_____ 3. The Aztecs had a good hybrid of amaranth.

_____ 4. Cortés hated amaranth and all it represented.

_____ 5. Some varieties of amaranth taste like spinach.

_____ 6. An important use of amaranth is in baked goods.

_____ 7. If we don't know when a crop will be harvested, we don't know what its height will be.

_____ 8. Hybrids mature faster than either parent.

_____ 9. Most countries don't want to buy amaranth.

_____ 10. It will probably be very expensive to grow and harvest amaranth.

Vocabulary in Context

EXERCISE

G. In each category cross out the unrelated word or phrase.

1. environment/farm expert/agriculturist
2. hybrid/trait/offspring
3. uncultivated/wild/adaptable
4. heavy/nutritious/high in protein
5. crackers/vegetable greens/baked goods
6. expected/probable/uniform
7. hardy/vigorous/feasible
8. lysine/amino acid/seed

COMPREHENSION SKILL INDEX

Uses of the Word *It*

The word *it* sometimes causes comprehension problems. It is important to have a thorough understanding of the many uses of this word in English.

Use 1

It is used as a pronoun instead of a neuter noun (a noun which names an inanimate object, an abstract idea, or, infrequently, a small child or animal). The noun may or may not have been mentioned previously.

examples: The book is about science. It is not about mathematics. (*It* = book)

Science is my main interest. It is also my best subject. (*It* = science)

Science is my main interest. I know a lot about it. (*It* = science)

Her research project was on some aspect of genetics. I'm not sure what it was. (*It* = some aspect)

The amoeba is a one-celled organism. It reproduces by dividing in two parts. (*It* = amoeba.)

Use 2

It is used as a part of many English idiomatic and impersonal expressions related to distance, the weather, time, and other subjects.

examples: It is hot in the tropics.

It rains from May to October.

It was snowing last week when we got there.

It is three o'clock.

It will be dark in an hour.

It will be three months before we know the results of the test.

It is 4,200 kilometers from Caracas to Hudson Bay.

It costs a lot to do research.

Use 3

It is used to anticipate the true subject or object of the sentence. In this use *it* has no translatable meaning. Note that this use of the word *it* sometimes enables the writer to avoid having to write two sentences to present the same idea.

examples: It is known that plaque builds up on artery walls. (*It* = that which is known, namely: that plaque builds up on artery walls.) This means: Plaque builds up on artery walls. This is known .

It has been shown that laser surgery is painless. (*It* = that which has been shown, namely: that laser surgery is painless.) This means: Laser surgery is painless. This has been shown.

It has been discovered that amaranth is nutritious. (*It* = that which has been discovered, namely: that amaranth is nutritious.) This means: Amaranth is nutritious. This has been discovered.

It is essential to understand genetics if you want to work on hybridization. (*It* = that which is essential, namely: to understand genetics.) This means: To understand genetics is essential if you want to work on hybridization.

It costs a lot to attend the university. (*It* = that which costs a lot, namely: to attend the university.) This means: To attend the university costs a lot.

It is true that it takes a long time to breed a wild plant into a major food crop. (*It* = that which is true, namely: that it takes a long time to breed a wild plant into a major food crop.) This means: To breed a wild plant into a major food crop takes a long time. This is true.

It is to her that we must write. (*It* = to whom we must write, namely: to her. This means: We must write to her.)

Uses of the Word It

EXERCISES

H. The reading selection on pages 69-70 contains the word *it* sixteen different times in fifteen sentences. Circle the word *it* each time it appears. Copy the fifteen sentences below.

1. _____

_____

2. _____

_____

3. _____

_____

4. _____

_____

5. _____

_____

6. _____

_____

7. _____

_____

8. _____

_____

9-10. _____

_____

11. _____

_____

12. _____

_____

13. _____

_____

14. _____

_____

15. _____

_____

16. _____

_____

I. In each of the blank spaces below, which correspond to the sixteen times *it* is used in exercise H, indicate whether the word *it* has use 1, use 2, or use 3 as outlined on pages 72-73 of this text.

1. _____   9. _____

2. _____   10. _____

3. _____   11. _____

4. _____   12. _____

5. _____   13. _____

6. _____   14. _____

7. _____   15. _____

8. _____   16. _____

J. Choose the correct lettered response to explain what *it* refers to in the following sentences taken from the reading.

1. Today only a few wild and uncultivated species of amaranth exist, and it is rarely used as a food in Mexico.
   a. *it* = amaranth
   b. *it* = food
   c. *it* = Mexico

2. It is true that breeding a wild plant into a major food crop such as wheat requires much research time.
   a. *it* = research time
   b. *it* = that which is true (breeding a wild plant into a major food crop such as wheat)
   c. *it* = wild plant

A farmer plants new corn directly into the rows left by the previous year's crop.

USDA, SCS Photo by Joe Branco

3. Agriculturists know that it has taken hundred of years of breeding different varieties of corn to get the kinds we have today.
   a. *it* = that which has taken hundreds of years (breeding different varieties of corn to get the kinds we have today)
   b. *it* = that which we get (the kinds of corn we have today)
   c. *it* = agriculturists

4. Because it is a wild plant, amaranth is difficult to grow commercially.
   a. *it* = wild plant
   b. *it* = amaranth
   c. *it* = that which we grow commercially

5. Does the crop require special machinery to harvest it?
   a. *it* = machinery
   b. *it* = the harvest
   c. *it* = the crop

6. It may be that in countries that are short of an adequate food supply, amaranth is the foodstuff of the future.
   a. *it* = that which may be (that amaranth is the foodstuff of the future
   b. *it* = countries that are short of an adequate food supply
   c. *it* = that which countries are short of (an adequate food supply)

Sharks: Their Physiology and Their Role in Cancer Research

The great white shark is one of the most ferocious inhabitants of the sea.

Subtechnical Vocabulary

to feed on (phrasal verb)

to eat

Many sea animals **feed on** microscopic organisms that live around them.

to wear out (phrasal verb)

to use completely; to be diminished by use

You **can wear out** your shoes by walking great distances.

to pick up (phrasal verb)

to detect

A seismograph **picks up** and records earthquakes that occur far away.

to rid [oneself of] (phrasal verb)

to lose voluntarily

You may need an operation **to rid yourself of** arterial plaque.

to replace (verb)

to supply again; to put (something) in the place of (something else)

It is necessary **to replace** car parts that have worn out.

to aid (verb)

to help

Reducing wind resistance **aids** in increasing gas mileage.

to alert (verb)

to warn; to indicate that danger is near

A buildup of stress **alerts** us to the possibility of an earthquake.

to inhibit (verb)

to prevent; to slow

Antiseptics **inhibit** the growth of bacteria.

to attack (verb)

to begin to use force against (someone or something)

Antibiotics **attack** many bacteria and kill them.

ferocious (adjective)

>cruel, violent, savage

>Lions and tigers are **ferocious** animals.

set (noun)

>several things of the same kind meant to be used together

>Every laboratory scientist has a **set** of test tubes.

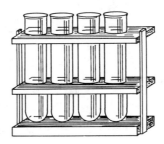

row (noun)

>a group of things in a line

>Corn is always planted in **rows**.

pit (noun)

>a depression in the skin or other surface

>Many poisonous snakes have **pits** near their eyes.

field (noun)

>an area with a measurable and specific force contained at every point, for example, a gravitational field or an electrical field

>In a magnetic **field** there are north and south poles.

gill (noun)

opening in a fish's body through which it breathes

The **gill** is the respiratory organ of the fish.

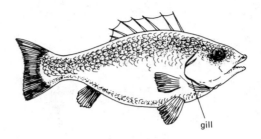

gill

cycle (noun)

one completed occurrence of an action which occurs repeatedly

Electrical current is measured in **cycles**.

frequency (noun)

the number of vibrations in a unit of time

In electricity **frequency** is a measure of the number of cycles of current per second.

prey (noun)

any animal taken by another to be eaten

The catching of **prey** seems cruel to us.

agent (noun)

material capable of performing a function

Chlorine is an **agent** for cleaning.

plankton (noun)

microscopic plants and animals that exist in the water

Many animals in the sea feed on **plankton**.

Vocabulary of Ideas

to conclude (verb)

to reach an idea after research or logical thinking

Many scientists **have concluded** that reducing fat in the diet aids in reducing the risk of heart attacks.

to be known to [do something] (phrasal verb)

> to have been observed to (do something)

> Many wild animals **are known to prey on** animals larger than they are.

to take a look [at] (phrasal verb)

> to study

> Scientists **are taking a look at** all the possible uses of lasers.

a number of

> several or many

> Lasers have **a number of** new uses.

up to [a number]

> almost, or sometimes reaching (a number)

> This car gets **up to 20** kilometers per liter of gasoline.

about (adverb)

> approximately

> There are **about** 250 species of wild plants that have yellow flowers.

Thought Connectors: Expressions of Contrast

although

> **Although** laser surgery looks promising, many of the newer uses have only been tried on animal patients.

but

> Sharks are generally not ferocious, **but** they can be very unpredictable.

however

> Amaranth is a nutritious and hardy plant. Its widespread commercial use, **however**, is still questionable.

in contrast

> Older cars wasted a lot of fuel. **In contrast,** the newer, aerodynamically designed cars get better gas mileage.

on the other hand

This professor has not published any original scientific research, and she is not generally recognized to be a leader in her field. **On the other hand**, she is the best teacher in the department.

unlike

Unlike surgery, laser repair cannot cause bleeding.

while

While earthquakes can be very destructive, it is not necessary to live in fear of them.

Vocabulary Exercises

A. Choose the correct lettered response to complete each numbered statement.

1. A group of things arranged in a straight line is a _____.
   a. set
   b. row
   c. corn
   d. field

2. Ferocious animals _____ their prey.
   a. inhibit
   b. attack
   c. replace
   d. aid

3. A _____ can be an irregularity in the surface of the skin.
   a. pit
   b. gill
   c. cycle
   d. plankton

4. In very sick people the heartbeat is often difficult to _____.
   a. alert
   b. aid
   c. wear out
   d. pick up

5. Smoke is known to be a cancer-causing _____.
   a. agent
   b. prey
   c. field
   d. cycle

6. Frequency and _____ are two words associated with electricity.
    a. gill
    b. set
    c. cycle
    d. aid

7. Wind tunnel studies _____ car designers to specific areas of drag.
    a. alert
    b. take a look at
    c. aid
    d. conclude

8. Earthquakes with high readings on the Richter scale are _____ to cause severe damage.
    a. aided
    b. concluded
    c. known
    d. inhibited

9. Very cold weather can _____ the growth of food crops.
    a. rid oneself of
    b. take a look at
    c. feed on
    d. inhibit

10. Almost every animal species is _____ to some other species.
    a. plankton
    b. agent
    c. prey
    d. gill

B. Unscramble the cue word in column b to match it with its definition in column a.

a	*b*
1. microscopic sea life	SOOFURICE
2. similar objects used together	KLONPANT
3. not kind, gentle, or tame	UTOBA
4. resupply	DIA
5. assist	TSE
6. more or less	LACREPE

C. Mark the following statements T if they are true or F if they are false.

_____ 1. When you rid yourself of something, you get more of it.

_____ 2. Taking a look at something sometimes means studying it.

_____ 3. Gills are organs for underwater respiration.

_____ 4. A field is an area.

_____ 5. When something wears out, it is in better condition than it was in the past.

_____ 6. Frequency is a word of measurement.

_____ 7. If someone concludes something, it means he or she has thought about the subject.

_____ 8. If you are told to take up to eight aspirins a day, you should not take more than eight.

_____ 9. To feed on something means to give it food.

_____ 10. A number of ideas means several ideas.

COMPREHENSION SKILL INDEX | Scanning

Another important reading skill is scanning. Unlike skimming, which gives you a general, overall view of a reading, scanning helps you find specific information you want. Scanning is a skill you will want to use when you know what information a text contains and you want to find answers to specific questions you have about that subject.

Scanning is used, therefore, to enable you either to read selectively or to read to find specific information only. After skimming to get the general idea and content of a text from its title, subheads, and topic sentences, you either (1) read only those paragraphs that are of interest to you or (2) read the whole body of the text, concentrating only on specific facts of interest to you.

Scanning

EXERCISES

D. Skim the reading on pages 86-87. Then copy the probable topic sentences.

1. _____

_____

2. _____

_____

3. _____

_____

4. _____

_____

5. _____

_____

Now look at the following topics of interest. Indicate to the left of each topic the paragraph in which you would probably find information about that topic.

Paragraph
Number

_____ 6. the shark's teeth

_____ 7. the shark's ability to think and feel

_____ 8. a description of the various kinds of sharks

_____ 9. the directions shark research will take

E. Scan paragraph 3. It contains eight facts about shark teeth. Underline and number the facts 1 to 8, and write them in the space provided below.

1. _____

_____

2. _____

_____

3. _____

_____

4. _____

_____

5. _____

_____

6. _____

_____

7. _____

_____

8. _____

_____

A shark swims with a parasitic sucker fish attached to its side.

American Museum of Natural History

Reading Selection

Sharks: Their Physiology and Their Role in Cancer Research

Sharks have lived on earth for more than 180 million years. **Although** they live in all the oceans of the world, they are found mostly in subtropical and tropical waters.

1

waters: oceans

There are **about** 350 species of sharks. The largest sharks are the whale shark and the basking shark, which **feed on plankton** and small fish. The adult whale shark grows to about 13 meters long, **while** the basking shark extends a little over 8 meters. Most of the species are not particularly **ferocious. On the other hand**, there are **a number of** them which **have attacked** and killed swimmers. These sharks include mako, the great hammerhead, lemon, blue, whitetip, and, of course, the great white shark. The great white is the largest and most ferocious of all animals **known to** attack humans. The great white grows to between 5 and 8 meters long and can weigh more than 1,300 kilograms. It can swim through the water at speeds reaching 32 kilometers per hour. **However,** one of the fastest swimmers in the shark family is the blue shark, which can swim at a speed of nearly 72 kilometers per hour.

2

reaching: up to

Physiology of Sharks

One of the most unusual aspects of the shark is its teeth. They can grow as long as 5 centimeters, and they are razor sharp. **Unlike** humans, who have two **sets** of teeth in their lifetime, some sharks can have as many as five or six sets. It is rare for a shark to have fewer than four sets. As the shark's teeth **are worn out**, they fall out and **are replaced** by the next **row.** Some sharks can wear out a full set of teeth in less than six months. In a lifetime some sharks can grow and lose between 10,000 and 30,000 teeth.

3

marine: related to
the sea

snout: nose

navigation: knowing
where to go

lateral: on its sides

Marine biologists have discovered that the shark has a remarkably large brain and a well-developed sensory system. The animal has an extraordinary sense of smell and excellent vision. **But** sharks are also sensitive to electrical **fields.** Special sensory **pits** on the shark's snout and chin can detect weak electrical fields in the water that are produced by fish and other animals. For example, the **gill** action of a flounder can produce **frequencies** of **up to** eight **cycles** per second, which can be detected by the shark's sensory pits. Scientists **have concluded** that sharks associate food with electrical fields. Scientists also believe that sharks create their own electrical field **to aid** them in navigation. In addition to the sensory pits in the shark's snout, the shark also has a lateral sensory system that runs along the length of its body. Sounds made by fish and other **prey can be picked up** by this sensory system, **alerting** the shark.

4

Shark Studies and Cancer

in hopes of: in
order to

bony: with
skeleton of bone,
not cartilage

as well as: and

Marine biologists are **taking a closer look at** the physiology of the shark in hopes of finding clues that may help fight cancer in humans. Scientists have found that sharks, **in contrast** to bony fish, do not develop cancer. The shark's blood seems **to inhibit** the growth of cancer as well as bacteria and viruses. Scientists are now testing the blood to find out how the shark **rids itself of** cancer-producing **agents.** It is hoped that this discovery can be applied in human cancer prevention and treatment.

5

Comprehension

EXERCISE

F. Choose the correct lettered response to answer each of the following questions.

1. How long have sharks lived on earth?
   a. about 30 meters long
   b. more than 180 million years
   c. as long as 5 centimeters

2. Where do sharks live?
   a. in all seas
   b. mostly in colder waters
   c. every place on the earth

3. Which are the largest sharks?
   a. the basking shark and plankton
   b. the great white shark and the great hammerhead
   c. the whale shark and the basking shark

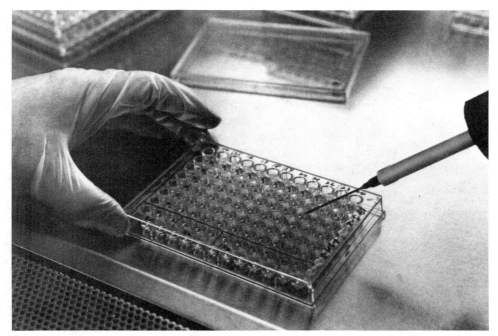

Cancer researchers study the effect of interferon on cancer virus.
American Cancer Society

4. What is the length of the adult whale shark?
   a. about 13 meters
   b. a little over 8 meters
   c. more than 180 million years

5. Which sharks have attacked humans?
   a. all species
   b. mako, blue, and great white
   c. basking shark and the whale shark

6. How long is the great white shark adult?
   a. up to 8 meters long
   b. more than 1,300 kilograms
   c. up to 32 kilometers per hour

7. How long are the shark's teeth?
   a. less than six months
   b. as many as five or six sets
   c. up to 5 centimeters long

8. How fast can some sharks use up a full set of teeth?
   a. in less than six months
   b. at speeds reaching 32 kilometers per hour
   c. between 10,000 and 30,000 teeth

9. What do sharks have?
   a. only one set of teeth
   b. weak electrical fields
   c. a large brain and good vision and sense of smell

10. What organ in the shark picks up electrical fields in the water?
    a. the flounder's gills
    b. special sensory pits at the front end of the animal
    c. the teeth

11. What probably helps the shark navigate?
    a. its own electrical field
    b. its lateral sensory system
    c. its sensory pits

12. Why are people studying the shark's physiology?
    a. to aid in human cancer research
    b. to prevent sharks from getting cancer
    c. to take a closer look

Vocabulary in Context

EXERCISE

G. Mark the following statements T if they are true or F if they are false.

_____ 1. Sharks are land animals.

_____ 2. Physiology involves the body and how it works.

_____ 3. A flounder is a fish.

_____ 4. A marine biologist is a specialist in life on land.

COMPREHENSION SKILL INDEX

Words and Expressions of Contrast

Writers help you understand or remember what they write by contrasting what is probably new to the reader with what is probably familiar to the reader.

example: Unlike laser surgery, which can be performed in a doctor's office, traditional surgery must be performed in a hospital because of the danger of complications.

Words and expressions of contrast can aid you in understanding a sentence that contains words you do not know. If you understand the words of contrast, you may guess the meaning of the unknown word or words.

example: Most strong earthquakes in lonely outposts are not dangerous. On the other hand, even a fairly minor one in a city can cause great damage.

Even if you never saw the expression "lonely outposts" before, the expression "on the other hand" is a clue to the meaning of the unknown words. You can understand from this contrast that a lonely outpost is very different from a city, and therefore must mean a relatively uninhabited place.

When you read, it is a good idea to pay particular attention to words and expressions of contrast. They will help you better understand and appreciate the reading, and will save you unnecessary time with the dictionary.

Some common expressions of contrast are *while, however, unlike, but, although, in contrast,* and *on the other hand.*

examples: Sharks have a cartilaginous skeleton, while bony fish have a skeleton made of bone. (Contrast: skeleton. Explanation: There is something unusual about the shark's skeleton. It is unlike that of other fish.)

Earthquakes occur most frequently in the western part of the United States. However, they also occur in all parts of North America. (Contrast: earthquake locations. Explanation: You probably already know that earthquakes occur in the West. You probably do not know that they also occur in Nova Scotia.)

Amaranth and other wild plants can be hard to farm because, unlike corn, wheat, and oats, they do not have a known harvest time. (Contrast: harvest times for various grains. Explanation: The reason amaranth is hard to farm is that it doesn't have a predictable harvest time.)

Most eye surgery is still performed in the traditional manner. But more and more conditions are beginning to be treated with lasers, making true surgery unnecessary. (Contrast: surgical methods. Explanation: The reality of the situation is that lasers have not made eye surgery a thing of the past.)

Although studies have shown an association between high blood lipid levels and arterial plaque, many scientists feel the relationship is not yet entirely understood. (Contrast: assumptions and proven fact. Explanation: There is still controversy about this subject.)

The English system of measurement is based on multiples of twelve. In contrast, the metric system is always based on multiples of ten. (Contrast: systems of measurement. Explanation: See just how different two systems of measurement can be.)

Having an advanced degree in science does not help a teacher teach. On the other hand, it is impossible to get a science teaching position wthout having an advanced degree in science. (Contrast: methods of preparing for teaching. Explanation: Absurdity of situation pointed out.)

Words and Expressions of Contrast

EXERCISE

H. The following sentences from the reading each contain some new information or a surprise indicated or introduced by an expression of contrast. Choose the explanation that best indicates the surprise or the new information.

1. Although they live in all the oceans of the world, they are found mostly in sub-tropical and tropical waters.
   a. They are found in equal numbers in all the world's oceans.
   b. They are found more often in warmer seas.

2. The adult whale shark grows to about 13 meters long, while the basking shark extends a little over 8 meters.
   a. In the same period of time, the whale shark grows much more.
   b. These are two big sharks. One is even bigger than the other.

3. Most of the species are not particularly ferocious. On the other hand, there are a number of them which have attacked and killed swimmers.
   a. Only some sharks are ferocious.
   b. Sharks like to bite swimmers' hands.

4. It can swim through the water at speeds reaching 32 kilometers. However, one of the fastest swimmers in the shark family is the blue shark, which can swim at a speed of nearly 72 kilometers.
   a. Sharks generally swim slowly. The blue shark in an exception.
   b. Even though 32 kilometers per hour is very fast, the blue shark can swim more than twice as fast.

5. Unlike humans, who have two sets of teeth in their lifetime, some sharks can have as many as five or six sets.
   a. Five or six sets seems like a lot of sets, because we are humans and are accustomed to two sets.
   b. The shark doesn't have two sets of teeth.

6. The animal has an extraordinary sense of smell and excellent vision. But sharks are also sensitive to electrical fields.
   a. The sensitivity to electrical fields damages the shark's sense of smell and hearing.
   b. Even though the animal has an extraordinary sense of smell, that is not all. It has yet another sense.

7. Scientists have found that sharks, in contrast to bony fish, do not develop cancer.
   a. This is one way sharks differ from bony fish.
   b. Bony fish and sharks do not develop cancer.

Comparative, Superlative, and other Expressions of Comparison

Review the construction of simple, comparative, and superlative adjectives.

examples:

With *-er, est*

simple	*comparative*	*superlative*
wild	wilder	wildest

The shark is as wild as the lion.
Amaranth is wilder than corn.
The wildest plants are the hardest to grow.

With *more, most*

ferocious	more ferocious	most ferocious

Some species are not as (so) ferocious as others.
Reptiles are more ferocious than amoebas.
Lions are the most ferocious cats.

Irregular Forms

bad	worse	worst
badly	worse	worst
good	better	best
well	better	best
far	farther, further	farthest, furthest
little	less	least
much	more	most
many	more	most

This car gets as good gas mileage as that car.
Sharks swim farther than amoebas.
Blindness is the worst thing that can happen to an eye.

Other Expressions of Comparison

over (more than)   A fever is a temperature of **over** 37°C.
mostly (most commonly)   This airline's planes consist **mostly** of jets.

same	Thirty-two degrees Fahrenheit is the **same** as 0° Celsius.
alike	These two cars are **alike** in price, but not in quality.
equal	Some people believe that breathing heavily polluted air is **equal** to smoking a pack of cigarettes day.
like	Sharks are **like** bony fish in their ability to swim, but unlike them in their anatomy.
similar	Wheat and corn are able to grow in **similar** conditions.
different	Laser surgery is **different** from traditional surgery in many ways.
superior	Amaranth is **superior** to many other food crops because it is hardier.
inferior	At present traditional surgery for retina reattachment is **inferior** to laser repair.

"the (comparative) . . . the (comparative)"   The **more** you study, the **more** you learn.

Comparative, Superlative, and Other Expressions of Comparison

EXERCISES

I. Find fifteen sentences that express a comparison in the reading on pages 86-87.

1. _____

_____

A view of the interior of a shark's mouth shows its teeth.
American Museum of Natural History

2. _____

_____

3. _____

_____

4. _____

_____

5. _____

_____

6. _____

_____

7. _____

_____

8. _____

_____

9. _____

_____

10. _____

_____

11. _____

_____

12. _____

_____

13. _____

_____

14. _____

_____

15. _____

_____

Photovoltaic Cells and Their Use as an Alternate Source of Energy

This flexible solar cell is adaptable to consumer use.

Subtechnical Vocabulary

antenna (noun)

a metal device for sending and receiving waves

A television **antenna** is usually placed on the roof of the house.

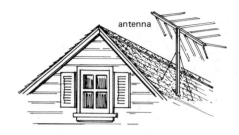

antenna

consumption (noun)

use, especially in a complete and final sense, such as of food, fuel, time, and so on

The **consumption** of cereal grains has decreased in the developed countries.

cell (noun)

a container with the necessary items to produce electricity

A car's battery is a **cell**.

wire (noun)

a thin, threadlike piece of metal used for tying things and carrying electricity

Electricity reaches light bulbs through **wires**.

base (noun)

the supporting part at the bottom of some manufactured objects

Generally, the larger the **base**, the more stable the object.

base

diameter (noun)

the length of the longest straight line from one outer edge to another outer edge of an object, usually of a circle or a sphere

The **diameter** of a circle is measured from one point on the circumference to another through the center.

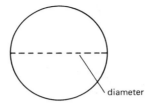

orbit (noun)

the path of one body in a field of force around another body

The earth travels in an **orbit** around the sun.

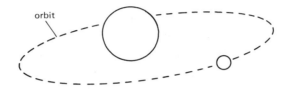

breakthrough (noun)

an important discovery or invention that changes everything for the better

The discovery of insulin was a **breakthrough** in diabetes treatment.

resource (noun)

available supply, for example, natural resources: air, water, gas, coal, and so on

Our natural **resources** must be used intelligently.

wing (noun)

the organ of flight; an object shaped like that organ

Airplanes have **wings**.

to dwindle (verb)

to become less, particularly a resource or other supply

When there is no rain for a long time, water supplies often **dwindle**.

to use up (phrasal verb)

to use until there is no more; to consume completely

After we **use up** all the coal on earth, there will be no more.

to transform (verb)

>to change into another form

>When fuel burns, it **is transformed** into energy.

to generate (verb)

>to create; to produce

>This power plant generates more energy than any other in the region.

to refine (verb)

>to make pure; to remove unrelated matter from a material

>Oil **is refined** from petroleum.

to convert (verb)

>to change; to transform

>Water power **is converted** to electricity.

to waste (verb)

>to fail to use something that should be used; to use something carelessly, and therefore incompletely

>Cars that are not aerodynamically designed **waste** a lot of fuel.

to launch (verb)

>to send into outer space; to send up

>When rockets **are launched**, they use enormous quantities of fuel.

launch

to renew (verb)

> to create or supply again

> The tanker arrived in time **to renew** the dwindling supply of oil in the region.

to distribute (verb)

> to divide a large amount into smaller amounts and give it to various people or put it in various places

> The bloodstream **distributes** oxygen to all the cells of the body.

to conduct (verb)

> to perform

> Research **is conducted** in all the major universities of the world.

to allow (verb)

> to permit

> The telephone **allows** us to talk to people far away without leaving home.

to stretch (verb)

> to extend

> The Atlantic Ocean **stretches** from Europe and Africa to the Americas.

alternate (adjective)

> other; another (sometimes) equally good or effective (thing)

> Alcohol is an **alternate** fuel for automobiles.

sufficient (adjective)

> enough

> We have **sufficient** gasoline to make the trip without refilling the tank.

currently (adverb)

> now; at present

> We **currently** do not know exactly what cancer-inhibiting agents are present in shark blood, but we hope to find out soon.

Vocabulary of Ideas

outlook (noun)

> what we may expect to see in the future; the prognosis

> Because of the new laser technology, the **outlook** is promising for patients with arterial plaque.

to consist (of) (verb)

  to be made of

  Water **consists** of hydrogen and oxygen.

to depend on (verb)

  to rely on; to be assured of; to expect support or aid

  Success in cancer treatment often **depends on** early discovery of the disease.

Vocabulary Exercises

A. Complete the following sentences with words from the list.

allowed	consisted	distributed	generated
dwindled	converted	launched	conducted
wasted	depended on	used up	stretched

1. Before laser surgery is approved for humans, very thorough animal studies must be

   _____.

2. Their diet _____ of grains, green vegetables, and fish.

3. Electricity is currently _____ indirectly by oil.

4. We have _____ our heating system from oil to natural gas.

5. Sales of slide rules have _____ because of the availability of pocket calculators.

6. After the earthquake, food and medical supplies were _____ to all residents of the area.

7. Most farmers have always _____ crops with predictable harvest times

8. The wind tunnel studies have _____ us to make design improvements in cars and airplanes.

9. Water and other natural resources are _____ each year because people don't think and plan.

B. Replace each italized word or expression with a synonym taken from the vocabulary in this lesson.

1. *At present* amaranth is being studied to see whether its cultivation can be made economically feasible.

2. The period of time needed to complete this study has been *extended* from three months to six months.

3. The diet of many people in poorer areas of the world does not supply *enough* protein.

4. It is essential to develop alternate energy sources before all our natural resources are *consumed.*

5. Windmills *convert* wind power to usable energy.

6. The *prognosis* for victims of advanced cancer is poor.

C. Cross out the incorrect italicized word in each of the following sentences.

1. Helicopters are able to fly without *wires/wings.*

2. The supporting part of an object is its *base/orbit.*

3. Good television reception often depends on having an *outlook/antenna.*

4. The electrons are in *diameter/orbit* around the nucleus of the atom.

5. Circles are measured by their *diameters/cells.*

6. Another good way to do something is an *allowed/alternate* way to do it.

7. When something is resupplied, it is *conducted/renewed.*

8. Nutritionists say we should not eat so many *refined/dwindled* foods.

9. A *cell/wire* is a place where electricity is created.

10. An important substance that should not be used up is a *resource/breakthrough.*

11. The government may decide to monitor the *diameter/consumption* of water during this dry period.

D. Puzzle

Make new words meaning a success, a sendoff, and a metal object by combining each word with the indicated letters. The new words you form come from the vocabulary list.

1. ROUGHBREAK + TH _ _ _ _ _ _ _ _ _ _ _ _

2. LUNCH + A _ _ _ _ _ _

3. IRE + W _ _ _ _

Understanding Vocabulary from Word Parts

Prefixes and Combining Forms

Beginning in this lesson there will be concentrated treatment of word parts: bases, prefixes, combining forms, and suffixes. Your ability to understand new words will greatly increase with an understanding of these elements.

English scientific and technical vocabulary is heavily derived from Greek and Latin roots. The following four words taken from the reading in this lesson illustrate the debt scientific English owes the classical languages:

examples: geothermal, (*geo* = earth, *thermal* = heat)

hydroelectric (*hydro* = water)

photovoltaic (*photo* = light)

refrigeration (*re* = again, *frig* = cold)

Prefixes are word parts used at the beginning of a word to make a new word or to change the meaning of the word. Often just knowing the meaning of the original word (base) and the meaning of the prefix will enable you to understand the longer word.

example: The word *unclean* means the opposite of *clean* because of the prefix, *un-*, meaning "not."

You already know many English words made up of prefixes, combining forms, and bases. In many cases you learned these words as a whole and gave no thought to their individual parts (*television*, for example). The following exercise will point out some common prefixes you already know.

Understanding Vocabulary from Word Parts: Prefixes and Combining Forms

EXERCISE

E. Choose the correct lettered response to complete each numbered statement. All the italicized words have been used in this text.

1. In *biology* and *biochemistry,' bio-* means _____.
   a. life
   b. two

2. In *inadequate, inanimate,* and *infrequently, in-* means _____.
   a. interior
   b. not

3. In *precede* and *predict, pre-* means _____.
   a. for
   b. before

4. In *replace, renew,* and *reproduce, re-* means _____.
   a. again
   b. strong

5. In *malnutrition, mal-* means _____.
   a. bad
   b. animal

6. In *circumference, circum-* means _____.
   a. facts
   b. around

7. In *bilingual, bi-* means _____.
   a. two
   b. snakelike

8. In *antibiotic, anti-* means _____.
   a. before
   b. against

Understanding Vocabulary from Word Parts

Prefixes and Combining Forms (continued)

It is important to remember that it is often not possible to guess the meaning of words even if you know the prefix or some other part of the word. This is because in many words the combination was made very long ago when the individual word parts had different meanings from the ones they have today. It is certainly easier to learn a hundred new English words than to interrupt your study to learn Greek and Latin! In other cases you may know the prefix but be unable to understand the whole word because the base word is obscure or used in a figurative sense.

example: The word *remorse* comes from the prefix *re-* meaning "again" and *mordere,* meaning "to bite." The word does not mean "to bite again," but rather refers to the feeling of emotional pain we have when thinking about our past mistakes. This beautiful word was coined because this sad feeling seems to bite us many times.

In spite of this sort of obscurity and archaic figurativeness, a good knowledge of word parts will be very helpful to the reader of science and technology because of the relative newness of many of the words common to these fields. If you do not already have a good knowledge of the most common English prefixes, study the following list.

examples: dis-, il-, im-, in-, ir-, mis-, non-, un-

Negative Prefixes

All the preceding prefixes serve to make the base word negative. There are some slight differences in meaning among the prefixes of this group. Examples of words with these prefixes are found in the general prefix list that follows:

General, High-Frequency Prefixes

a-	(without)	amoral
ab-	(not, away from)	abnormal
ante-	(before)	antedate
anti-	(against)	antibodies*
bi-	(two)	bilingual*

bio-	(life)	biochemistry*, biology*
circum-	(around)	circumference*, circumstance*
co-	(together)	coefficient*
counter-	(against)	counteract
contra-	(against)	contradict, contraindicate, controversy*
dis-	(not)	discover*, disagreement*
ex-	(former)	ex-chairman
ex-	(out of)	exposed*, exterior*
extra-	(outside)	extraordinary*, extraterrestrial
fore-	(before)	foresee*
il-	(not)	illogical
im-	(not)	impossible
in-	(not)	inadequate*, infrequently*
infra-	(below)	infrared
inter-	(between)	interchangeable
intra-	(within)	intramuscular
ir-	(not)	irregular*
macro-	(big)	macrosystem
mal-	(bad)	malnutrition*
mega-	(big)	megahertz
meta-	(beyond, changed)	metastasis
micro-	(small)	microscope*
mid-	(middle)	midair
mini-	(small)	minicar
mis-	(not)	miscalculate
multi-	(many)	multinational*
non-	(not)	nonreader*, nonsurgical*
over-	(more than necessary)	overcome*, overlearn
poly-	(many)	polychromatic
post-	(after)	postpone, postpartum, postwar
pre-	(before)	precede*, predate, predict*
pro-	(in favor of)	procedure*, produce*
pseudo-	(false)	pseudoscience
re-	(again)	replace*, reproduce*
semi-	(part, half)	semitropical
sub-	(under, below)	substandard
super-	(above, over)	superhuman
supra-	(above, over)	supramolecular

trans-	(across)	transplant*, transport*
ultra-	(very, beyond)	ultrasound
un-	(not)	unhealthy*, unreal*
under-	(less than necessary)	underestimate

*word used in this text

Understanding Vocabulary from Word Parts: Prefixes and Combining Forms (continued)

EXERCISE

F. Choose the correct lettered response to complete each numbered statement.

1. A pseudopregnancy is a _____.
   a. real pregnancy
   b. false pregnancy

2. An antenatal occurrence _____.
   a. prevents birth
   b. takes place before birth

3. A subnormal temperature is _____.
   a. below normal
   b. above normal

4. To circumnavigate an object means _____ .
   a. to move around it
   b. to move across it

5. An antiseptic acts _____.
   a. against infection
   b. in favor of infection

6. If a doctor finds a precancerous condition, a cancer _____.
   a. has already been cured
   b. may develop in the future

7. Postoperative complications occur _____.
   a. after surgery
   b. during surgery

8. A problem that has been overstudied _____.
   a. has been studied more than necessary
   b. needs further study

9. Microsurgery involves _____.
   a. a small area of the body
   b. the whole body

10. A megalith is _____.
    a. small
    b. big

Photovoltaic modules provide energy to private homes.
© Solarex Corporation

Reading Selection

Photovoltaic Cells and Their Use as an Alternate Source of Energy

Today there is much concern with the earth's **dwindling resources**. Most of our energy sources, such as coal, petroleum, and natural gas, are **nonrenewable** resources. If the **consumption** of these energy sources continues at the present rate, we can foresee their **being used up**. For this reason, scientists are taking a closer look at **alternate** sources of power: nuclear, geothermal, hydroelectric, wind, and solar.   1

Although solar energy is **currently** used in many places to heat water, the technology for its use as a source of electricity is still in its infancy. Scientists are now looking into photovoltaics as a growing solar technology that will be one of the most valuable sources of power in the future.   2

Using Photovoltaic Cells

The sun's rays **can be transformed** into electricity by a photovoltaic **cell**. A photovoltaic cell is also known as a solar cell. At present photovoltaic cells are used to power everything from watches and calculators to telephones and orbiting satellites. On the   3 other hand, they are not yet in general use as a source of electrical power.

Most photovoltaic cells are made from a single silicon crystal. Silicon is a common chemical element found abundantly in the earth's crust in quartz (a compound of silicon and oxygen). Silicon makes good photovoltaic material because its electrons can easily be released to produce electricity. The silicon crystal is first laced with a metal grid, or network, of tiny **wires**, and is then placed on a thin metal **base**. A typical cell is a wafer about 7 centimeters to 8 centimeters in **diameter** and thinner than a human hair.

How does the photovoltaic cell **convert** the sun's rays into electricity? We know that each ray of sunlight **consists of** little packets of energy called photons. When the photons strike the atoms of the solar cell, their energy **allows** the electrons to break free. They break free of their **orbit** around the nucleus of the silicon atom. The steady stream of electrons, or electrical current, flows through the thin wires to an electric light, motor, or whatever. After they do their work, the electrons return to the base of the solar cell to be used again by the sun's rays. The amount of electric current each cell produces **depends on** the amount of sunlight that is available and the ability of the cell to produce electricity.

There are still problems to overcome before photovoltaic cells can be widely used **to generate** power. First, **refining** silicon to a pure enough state is difficult and consequently costly. For this reason, research **is being conducted** on other elements such as copper, selenide, and indium to see if their use might be less expensive. Second, a photovoltaic cell can ordinarily convert a maximum of 10 to 15 percent of the sun's rays into electricity. This means that 85 to 90 percent of the sun's energy **is wasted**. Therefore, to produce a **sufficient** amount of power, many cells must now be grouped together in large panels. Scientists hope to have a **breakthrough** soon, making the solar cell more efficient and cost effective.

Outlook for the Future

Many believers in photovoltaics are excited about plans for a new solar-powered satellite. The solar-powered satellite **will be launched** in the mid-1980s. It will be held in an orbit about 36,000 kilometers above the earth. The satellite will be placed in such an orbit that it will remain in total sunlight close to 100 percent of the time (unlike earth-bound solar cells that spend part of their time under clouds). The satellite will have gigantic solar cell panel **wings** that **will stretch** several kilometers. The solar panels will convert the sun's rays into electrical energy, which will then be transformed into microwaves and beamed to an earth-based **antenna**. The microwave energy will be converted directly into electrical current and **distributed** to power stations for use.

abundantly: in large quantities

wafer: thin, flat object

packets: packages (figurative)

panels: flat, boardlike constructions

earth-bound: which can't move from the earth

gigantic: superlarge

4

5

6

7

Comprehension

G. Mark the following statements T if they are true or F if they are false.

_____ 1. Coal, petroleum, and natural gas are energy sources.

_____ 2. Solar energy is not being used at present.

_____ 3. Electricity cannot be produced from sunlight.

_____ 4. Silicon is used in solar cells.

_____ 5. Quartz is a rare compound.

_____ 6. The silicon crystal needs special preparation for use in the photo-voltaic cell.

_____ 7. Because the cells are still inefficient, each single cell must be very large.

_____ 8. Photons are made up of packets of the sun's rays.

_____ 9. Normally the electron is in orbit around the nucleus.

_____ 10. It is difficult to make silicon very pure.

_____ 11. We know that copper will be easier to refine than silicon.

_____ 12. The solar-powered satellite will not move.

_____ 13. The solar-powered satellite will be very large.

_____ 14. The satellite will convert the solar power directly to electrical current.

_____ 15. Microwaves are very small.

Vocabulary in Context

EXERCISE

H. Choose the correct lettered response to define each of the following words.

1. laced (¶ 4)
   a. moved quickly
   b. implanted
2. grid (¶ 4)
   a. network
   b. sand

A solar domestic hot water system converts the sun's rays into heat energy.

DAS Solar, New York City & Hackensack, N.J.

3. cost effective (¶ 6)
   a. economically efficient
   b. price raising

4. satellite (¶ 7)
   a. earth-orbiting object
   b. large wing

5. beamed (¶ 7)
   a. sent in ray or wave form
   b. hit on the head

COMPREHENSION SKILL INDEX

Distinguishing Fact from Opinion

You have already had practice in confirming content; that is, in distinguishing what the author stated from what the author did not state. A related skill is distinguishing fact from opinion.

Opinions in scientific and technical writing, unlike those in everyday social conversation, are *educated* guesses. An opinion is arrived at after some study or observation has taken place. It has not yet been proved but might be in the future. A fact, on the other hand, may be demonstrated or has already been proved. Once proved, facts are accepted and considered to be true.

A pocket calculator uses solar cells as its power source.

Energy Conversion Devices, Inc.

Distinguishing Fact from Opinion

EXERCISE

I. Label the following statements O if they are opinions or F if they are facts.

_____ 1. Photovoltaic cells are made from silicon crystals.

_____ 2. Our natural resources will run out.

_____ 3. Solar energy is the most important of the alternate energy sources.

_____ 4. Copper, selenide, and indium will be more cost-effective than silicon.

_____ 5. Supplies of coal, petroleum, and natural gas are dwindling.

_____ 6. Photovoltaic cells are also known as solar cells.

_____ 7. Lasers might be used in silicon refinement.

_____ 8. Solar energy will be used in every home by the year 2000.

Drawing Conclusions

All the statements (sentences) in the reading on pages 106-107 are statements of fact. You have now had an opportunity to become familiar with the facts about photovoltaic cells and their possible use as an alternate energy source. From the facts presented by the author, you will now be able to draw some conclusions.

Drawing Conclusions

EXERCISE

J. Draw conclusions from the reading. Choose a or b to complete each numbered statement.

1. Clouds reduce the efficiency of earth-bound solar cells because _____.
   a. they prevent the sunlight from striking the cell
   b. they cannot produce electricity

2. Coal, petroleum, and natural gas _____.
   a. can be manufactured
   b. cannot be manufactured

3. Solar power is one of the best of the alternate energy sources because _____.
   a. its energy is free and cannot be used up
   b. it will make use of space-age technology

4. When photovoltaic technology is more efficient and cost-effective, _____.
   a. it will probably be made more available for general use
   b. we will stop wasting our natural resources

5. The author seems to hope that _____.
   a. we will stop using electricity until solar power is available
   b. solar power will help us conserve our resources

LESSON SEVEN

Earth Resources Technology Satellites

Landsat-D, the fourth of the Landsat series, carries the multispectral scanner and a thematic mapper for greater accuracy.

Subtechnical Vocabulary

to equip (verb)

> to provide the necessary tools
>
> All cars **should be equipped** with side mirrors.

to overlap (verb)

> to cover one another partially; to stretch into the area occupied by another object
>
> When two papers **overlap,** it is difficult to read the one on the bottom.

to scan (verb)

> to detect and record details from a large area
>
> New machines **scan** entire organs in the body to look for abnormalities.

to identify (verb)

> to detect, recognize, and perhaps name
>
> The cancer-inhibiting factor in the shark's blood has not yet been **identified.**

to emerge (verb)

> to come out; to become visible
>
> The shark **emerged** from behind the rock and frightened the diver.

to standardize (verb)

> to make something conform with a known and accepted scale
>
> Tests **can be standardized** for judging large numbers of people.

to expand (verb)

> to get larger; to grow
>
> It is clear that the medical use of lasers **will be expanded** in the future.

to sort out (phrasal verb)

>to separate various parts of the whole

>In deciding which crops to plant in this soil, it is important **to sort out** those plants that grow best in an acid medium.

spectrum (noun)

>the distribution of energy emitted by light arranged in the order of wavelengths

>Red, orange, yellow, green, blue, and violet light form the visible **spectrum.**

pattern (noun)

>a characteristic arrangement of things; a characteristic way of doing things; a repetitive, predictable series of actions

>From an airplane, farmlands have a checkerboard **pattern.**

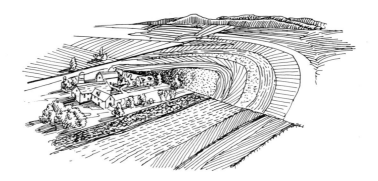

image (noun)

>picture; a visible reproduction of an object, particularly by a lens or in a mirror

>In a movie, **images** are projected on a large screen so that many people can see the film at the same time.

signal (noun)

the sound, message, or image sent or received in television, radio, and so on

It is difficult to get television reception in remote areas where the **signals** are weak.

shade (noun)

a variant of a color, caused by darkness or brightness

The laboratory was painted a light **shade** of green so that less energy would be used to light it.

blight (noun)

a general name for many plant diseases causing sudden death of the plant.

Botanists study ways to prevent **blight** of food crops.

soil (noun)

the top layer of the earth's crust; the layer in which plants grow

Amaranth can grow in a variety of **soils.**

surveillance (noun)

watching; monitoring

In order to reduce air pollution, the government has a **surveillance** program on car fuel emissions.

bare (adjective)

uncovered, empty

Trees are **bare** after the leaves fall off.

potential (adjective)

possible at a later time

A **potential** postsurgical complication is infection.

Vocabulary of Ideas

sequential (adjective)

occurring in order or sequence, one after the other

These ten photographs are **sequential** and were taken over a ten-day period.

unique (adjective)

> unlike any other
>
> Laser surgery is **unique** among surgical methods because it is the only one in which bleeding does not occur.

somewhat (adverb)

> more or less
>
> Scientists think that copper can be used in **somewhat** the same way as silicon, only for less money.

feature (noun)

> aspect; characteristic quality
>
> One of the most interesting **features** of the shark is its teeth.

Thought Connectors

therefore

> There is no food at home. **Therefore**, we have to go out if we want to eat.

consequently

> The rainstorm arrived this afternoon. **Consequently**, the university was closed for the rest of the day and evening.

for this reason

> Refining silicon to a pure state is difficult. **For this reason**, research is being conducted on copper.

first(ly), second(ly), and so on or **first of all, second of all, and so on**

> There are several reasons why amaranth is a promising crop for the world's poorer areas. **Firstly**, it can grow in a variety of soils. **Secondly**, it can grow in almost any temperate, subtropical, or tropical climate.

some examples or **as an example**

> There are many new uses for lasers. **Some examples** are retina reattachment, arterial plaque removal, and wind tunnel research.

in addition

> Shark blood seems to have some cancer-inhibiting agent. **In addition**, it seems to slow the growth of bacteria and viruses.

Vocabulary Exercises

A. Match each word in column a with its synonym in column b.

a	b
1. bare	grow
2. soil	monitoring
3. expand	picture
4. surveillance	dirt
5. image	empty

B. Choose the correct lettered response to complete each numbered statement.

1. When two objects overlap, they _____.
   a. cover each other
   b. come out

2. The distribution of energy from light is called the _____.
   a. spectrum
   b. pattern

3. If you provide persons with what they need for a specific job, you _____ them for the job.
   a. expand
   b. equip

4. Earthquake prediction is possible because of the _____ of stress buildup along faults.
   a. signal
   b. pattern

5. Pink is a _____ of red.
   a. shade
   b. feature

6. To make something conform to a recognized measurement is to _____.
   a. standardize it
   b. scan it

7. An instrument called a scanner probably _____ things.
   a. sorts out
   b. detects and records

8. In studying a problem, sometimes a pattern _____, making it easier to understand.
   a. emerges
   b. expands

9. _____ is a plant disease.
   a. Surveillance
   b. Blight

10. An earthquake is a _____ result of increased stress.
    a. sequential
    b. potential

11. An important _____ of some natural resources is that they are nonrenewable.
    a. spectrum
    b. feature

12. What you hear on the radio is sometimes generally referred to as the _____.
    a. signal
    b. image

13. The cause of many diseases is difficult to _____.
    a. identify
    b. standardize

C. Supply an appropriate word in the following sentences.

1. The shark's cancer-inhibiting agent appears to be _____ among fish.

2. Amaranth can be used in making bread in _____ the same way as wheat is.

3. In the spectrum the wavelengths are arranged in _____ length.

4. The periodic table _____ the chemical elements into groups determined by their properties.

COMPREHENSION SKILL INDEX

Understanding Vocabulary from Word Parts

Roots

In Lesson Six you had an opportunity to see how being familiar with prefixes can help you guess the meaning of new words.

Another class of word parts derived from Latin and Greek is used in a wide range of English science and technology vocabulary. The oldest science words in English used these roots, and even today, when new words are invented to describe new phenomena, we still use these recognizable Latin and Greek elements.

Study the following important word parts. The examples following each word part have all been used in Lessons One to Seven of this text.

examples:

ag, agri, agron (related to fields and soils)
agriculture
agriculturist
agronomist

geo (related to the planet earth)
geological
geology

phot, photo (related to light)
photosynthesis
photovoltaic

spec, spect (related to looking at or seeing)
aspect
multispectral
spectrum
speculate

The following exercise is not a test. The purpose of this exercise is to help you see how Latin and Greek word parts work together in English words.

Understanding Vocabulary from Word Parts: Roots

EXERCISES

D. Match each word in column a with its probable definition in column b.

a	*b*
1. specimen	having the shape or form of the earth
2. photograph	look at very closely
3. agrarian	study of the composition of the earth's crust
4. photobiotic	image recorded from shining light on a light-sensitive surface
5. inspect	related to land
6. geochemistry	sample of a material to be looked at closely
7. photophobic	needing light for life
8. geomorphic	abnormally uncomfortable from light

E. In an English dictionary find two more words using each of the following word parts. Put the words and their definitions in the space provided.

1. spec _____

_____

_____

2. geo _____

_____

_____

3. photo _____

_____

_____

A satellite image shows fruit orchards and vegetable fields in California's San Joaquin Valley. The number 4 indicates the San Andreas Fault.
NASA

Earth Resources Technology Satellites

The first earth resources technology satellite, Landsat, was launched in 1972. Since then this and several other Landsat satellites have taken thousands of pictures of the earth's surface. These pictures are helping us learn more about the earth—its mountains, vegetation, and bodies of water.

1

The Landsat spacecraft orbits the polar regions of the earth at a height of 920 kilometers. Once every 103 minutes the satellite makes a complete orbit of the earth. At this speed the satellite passes over the entire surface of the rotating earth in only eighteen days. The satellite is powered by photovoltaic cells in two solar panels which provide 500 watts of electrical energy for the orbiting craft.

2

Taking Pictures of Earth

The orbiting spacecraft is **equipped** with special instruments that are used to produce **sequential, overlapping** pictures of the surface of the earth. One of these instruments is called a multispectral **scanner**. This instrument is able to sense a wide variety of wavelengths emitted by reflected sunlight from the earth. Some of the wavelengths are from the bands of the visible **spectrum** that includes red, yellow, and blue. The invisible infrared spectrum is also sensed by the multispectral scanner. Since water, vegetation, and minerals each have **unique** identifying **patterns** in multispectral light, the scanner can **identify** differing **features** of the earth. **As an example,** the longer, infrared waves indicate temperature and, **therefore,** the possibility of life. One set of unchanging wavelengths is characteristic of water, another is indicative of vegetation, and so on. Particular combinations of wavelengths identify everything from streams and rivers to plains and mountains.

3

bands: the visible representation of the spectrum

plains: flat land areas

Multispectral Scanner Data Transmission

During its eighteen-day orbit Landsat records more than 30,000 scenes. Each scene is made up of 32 million tiny squares called picture elements, or "pixels." These satellite picture elements are transmitted to earth in **somewhat** the same way that a television station sends "pictures" to your home. The receiving stations on earth convert the **emerging** picture elements into **images** in a method similar to the way your television converts electrical signals into a picture. The images are turned into black-and-white or color pictures. The color pictures are in "false" colors; that is, certain objects are shown in colors other than their natural ones. As an

4

example, **bare** ground appears white or light gray. Water is black or dark blue. Vegetation appears in varying **shades** of red. This **standardized** coloring system was developed to assist scientists in image interpretation.

Uses of Landsat Imagery

More than 130 countries are currently receiving pictures from the Landsat satellites. The pictures can be very valuable and can be used to make more accurate maps. Geologists study lineaments in the pictures. Lineaments are land structures that form raised or depressed areas. One example of a lineament is a geological fault in the earth's crust. The Landsat satellite detects lineaments on the earth's surface very clearly. Studying lineaments is important because mineral **deposits** such as uranium and petroleum are located on or near the lineaments. Agronomists and farmers use the pictures to study crops. Each crop has a slightly different color, detectable by the satellite. Viewers **sort out** the different colors and determine the name of the crop, where it is, and how many hectares of it there are. **In addition**, the pictures can indicate which crops are ready for harvest, or they can serve as an early warning system of **potential** damage to these renewable resources. **Some examples** of potentially damaging conditions are insect infestation and corn **blight**. Landsat pictures are also being used to monitor water pollution, analyze droughts, and study **soil** conditions. Scientists predict the **expanding** use of earth resource technology satellites for future natural resource **surveillance.**

5

droughts: periods of little or no rainfall

Comprehension

EXERCISE

F. Mark the following statements T if they are true or F if they are false.

_____ 1. The first earth resources technology satellite was put into orbit in 1972.

_____ 2. Landsat flies at an altitude of 920 kilometers.

_____ 3. The spacecraft makes a complete orbit every eighteen days.

_____ 4. The solar cells provide energy for Landsat itself.

_____ 5. The instruments aboard Landsat take pictures of the earth.

_____ 6. The instruments identify the earth's different features by emitting unique patterns.

_____ 7. Infrared waves are used to detect underground objects that are invisible to the eye.

_____ 8. Pixels are very small parts of a very large image.

_____ 9. Pixels are made into understandable pictures by being converted into images by earth-based receiving stations.

_____ 10. In the standardized coloring system, vegetation is red.

_____ 11. A wide range of people all over the world are interested in Landsat data.

_____ 12. Lineaments are mineral deposits.

_____ 13. Earth resources technology satellites will be used in the future to supply the earth with solar power.

Drawing Conclusions

EXERCISE

G. Draw conclusions from the reading. Choose a or b to complete each numbered statement.

1. Landsat covers the whole surface of the earth in eighteen days because _____.
   a. the earth rotates
   b. its orbit goes over Poland

2. One way Landsat differs from the satellite described in Lesson Six is that _____.
   a. its solar panels do not send power to earth
   b. they are both in orbit

3. The reason that Landsat imagery is so helpful to mapmakers is that _____.
   a. they are a recorded image of large areas and show land shapes accurately
   b. they allow for the rotation of the earth

4. The most important function of Landsat is probably _____.
   a. finding uranium
   b. monitoring the earth's natural resources

5. The reason Landsat pictures can serve as an early warning system for insect infestation is that _____.
   a. a large areawide picture can determine the size of the affected area and the direction in which the insects are moving
   b. insects cannot be seen from nearby

6. One way that crops differ from coal and petroleum is that _____.
   a. crops are renewable resources, while coal and petroleum are nonrenewable resources
   b. coal and petroleum are more valuable than crops

7. Another possible use of Landsat might be _____.
   a. detecting changes in the polar ice caps
   b. in cancer research

COMPREHENSION SKILL INDEX | **The Present Participle**

The -*ing* ending is very common in English. Three very different kinds of -*ing* words are progressive verbs, gerunds (see Lesson Two), and present participles.

examples:

                present perfect
                 progressive

1. Landsat has been orbiting the earth since 1972.

   gerund

2. Converting pixels into understandable images is the function of the receiving stations.

      present
      participle

3. The receiving stations convert pixels into understandable images.

Note that the -*ing* word in Sentence 1 functions as a verb. The phrase in which the -*ing* word occurs in Sentence 2 functions as a noun. The -*ing* word in Sentence 3 functions as an adjective. Present participles are verbal adjectives.

You will encounter present participles, gerunds, and progressive tense verbs throughout your scientific and technical readings. Being able to distinguish them from each other will help your reading comprehension because each of these uses of -*ing* words has a completely different meaning.

The Present Participle

EXERCISES

H. In the following sentences indicate whether the -*ing* word functions as a verb, a noun, or an adjective.

_____ 1. Reading is a specialized skill that requires practice.

_____ 2. Doctors are performing laser surgery in hospitals all over the world.

_____ 3. Our natural resources are being used up at an alarming rate.

_____ 4. A photovoltaic cell is simply a converting device.

_____ 5. One of the most important agricultural experiments is the growing of amaranth in marginal areas.

_____ 6. Marine biologists have been taking a closer look at the shark's blood.

_____ 7. Scanning for important details is useful if you want to save time.

_____ 8. This textbook is a reading text.

_____ 9. The beating heart is a sign of life.

_____ 10. Weighing is an essential feature of a physical examination.

_____ 11. The attacking shark was a great white.

_____ 12. She talks about participating in the seminar.

_____ 13. Our changing technology is always in the news.

_____ 14. Growing amaranth is beautiful to see.

_____ 15. In 1992 the first Landsat will have been orbiting the earth for twenty years.

I. The reading on pages 121-122 contains fourteen sentences with present participles. List them below in the space provided. Remember to distinguish these present participles from the gerunds and progressive verb forms which also appear in the same reading.

1. _____

_____

2. _____

_____

3. _____

_____

4. _____

_____

5. _____

_____

6. _____

_____

7. _____

_____

8. _____
_____
9. _____
_____
10. _____
_____
11. _____
_____
12. _____
_____
13. _____
_____
14. _____
_____

J. For each of the present participles in Exercise I, give the noun it describes in the reading.

1. _____
2. _____
3. _____
4. _____
5. _____
6. _____
7. _____
8. _____
9. _____
10. _____
11. _____
12. _____
13. _____
14. _____

Noun Compounds

You have already studied simple two- and three-word noun compounds and have seen how frequently they occur in English. English does not stop with these shorter noun groups. As you read more and more complex scientific texts, you will begin to see longer and longer noun compounds—sometimes including adjectives in their midst and often containing highly technical vocabulary.

example: Landsat imagery sequential conversion device

Remember that the key to understanding the longer and more technical compounds is the same as the key to understanding the shorter, simpler ones: Be sure which is the main, or most important, word. With the long compounds, as with the short ones, the most important noun is usually the last.

Noun Compounds

EXERCISE

K. The following two-, three-, and four-word noun compounds come from the reading on pages 121-122. Follow the model to practice understanding them.

example: Landsat satellites ⟶

What kind of satellites? *Landsat satellites*

1. Landsat satellites _____

_____

2. picture elements _____

_____

3. television stations _____

_____

4. color pictures _____

_____

5. insect infestation _____

_____

6. corn blight _____

_____

7. water pollution _____

_____

8. soil conditions _____

_____

9. satellite picture elements _____

_____

10. multispectral scanner data transmission _____

_____

11. earth resources technology satellites _____

_____

12. future natural resource surveillance _____

_____

Acid Rain: Its Effect on the Aquatic Ecosystem

Smokestacks in an industrial area of Germany release smoke and pollutants into the air.

Subtechnical Vocabulary

ecosystem (noun)

> the plants, animals, and environment in a particular place

> Poisonous wastes affect the **ecosystem.**

fossil (noun)

> body, body part, or mark left by an animal or plant that lived in the past, naturally preserved in the earth's crust

> **Fossils** are a record of the plants and animals of the past.

combustion (noun)

> burning

> Air is necessary for **combustion** to occur.

mass (noun)

> large body of some substance

> A polar air **mass** brought cold weather to this city yesterday.

particle (noun)

> a very small piece of a substance

> It is easy to have an insect infestation in a house where food **particles** are not cleaned up.

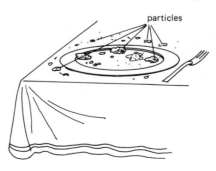

bonding (noun)

the process of permanent attachment by chemical or physical means

In chemical **bonding** the atoms are held together in a molecule or crystal.

$$H-\overset{\overset{H}{|}}{\underset{\underset{H}{|}}{C}}-\overset{\overset{H}{|}}{\underset{\underset{H}{|}}{C}}-H$$

chemical bond

moisture (noun)

humidity, water content

When the humidity is high, there is a lot of **moisture** in the air.

impact (noun)

effect; particularly a serious effect

A sudden decrease in moisture has a great **impact** on plants.

challenge (noun)

a difficult condition or problem that requires great work to resolve

The need to increase gas mileage is a new **challenge** to car designers.

mortality (noun)

death; death rate

Many new treatments have had an important impact on cancer **mortality**.

remedy (noun)

solution to a problem; treatment for an illness

The best **remedy** for headache is aspirin.

to eject (verb)

to throw off; to throw out; to release

In combustion gases **are ejected.**

to contaminate (verb)

to make dirty; to poison; to pollute

Our air **has been contaminated** by a variety of substances.

to suggest (verb)

>to indicate without stating directly
>
>Recent studies **suggest** that the cancer-inhibiting factor in the shark's blood may be unique to the shark.

to classify (verb)

>to characterize; to put a descriptive name to
>
>Amaranth **is** still **classified** as a wild plant.

to survive (verb)

>to live; to be capable of living even in difficult conditions
>
>Amaranth **can survive** in soils that less hardy plants die in.

to sustain (verb)

>to support, in the minimum sense; to give what is necessary to allow a living thing to survive
>
>Life **cannot be sustained** for long periods without water.

to convey (verb)

>to carry
>
>Airborne particles **can be conveyed** for long distances by moving air masses.

to interact (verb)

>to work together in order to cause a particular result
>
>In the combustion process fuel, heat, and air **interact** to cause burning.

to alter (verb)

>to change
>
>The volume of gas **is altered** by heat.

to threaten (verb)

>to menace; to indicate danger; to cause fear of harm or death
>
>The cold weather **has threatened** the tourist industry here this year.

airborne (adjective)

>carried by the air

Many **airborne** particles are harmless, but others, such as plant pollens, cause health problems for many people.

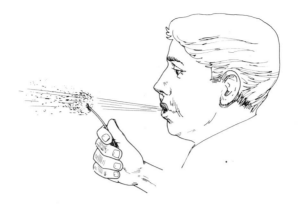

noxious (adjective)

> harmful, dangerous; poisonous
>
> The air and water are contaminated by **noxious** substances.

hazardous (adjective)

> dangerous to life
>
> Snow and rain often produce **hazardous** driving conditions.

extinct (adjective)

> no longer existing as a species; said of a life form that once existed but no longer does
>
> Dinosaurs are **extinct**.

considerable (adjective)

> important; significant; large in amount
>
> Long periods of cold weather can cause **considerable** danger to fruit crops.

Vocabulary of Ideas

issue (noun)

> a subject of controversy or discussion
>
> The **issue** of air pollution is relatively new in human history.

to lead to (phrasal verb)

> to cause in a step-by-step manner
>
> Drinking too much alcohol often **leads to** alcoholism.

on the decline

> dwindling; decreasing
>
> We hope that air pollution levels are now **on the decline**.

Thought Connectors

in spite of

> **In spite of** the precautions, combustion occurred and there was a terrible fire.

thus

> The shark was big and hungry, and **thus** dangerous.

furthermore

> Amaranth is nutritious and tastes good. **Furthermore**, it is the most promising of the wild plants because it is hardy enough to survive in challenging environments.

besides

> Lasers are a good substitute for eye surgery. **Besides**, their use is less costly than true operations.

moreover

> Air pollution and water pollution are hazardous consequences of modern life. **Moreover**, they are growing every day and threaten our very survival

nevertheless

> There is much hope that photovoltaics will help us one day to be less dependent on petroleum products. **Nevertheless**, that day is probably still in the remote future, and we must reduce our fuel consumption now.

as a result

> The cost of gasoline has increased considerably in the last few years. **As a result**, there has been a growing market for more fuel-efficient cars.

in conclusion

Silicon functions well in solar cells but is expensive. Research indicates that copper may be more promising. **In conclusion**, there are still uncertainties about which element will be most important in the future of photovoltaic technology.

Vocabulary Exercises

A. Choose a lettered synonym for the italicized term in each numbered statement.

1. Reducing the *moisture* in the environment inhibits the growth of many organisms.
   a. water content
   b. dryness
   c. pollutants
   d. people

2. The water supply in this region was *contaminated* with industrial pollutants.
   a. carried
   b. poisoned
   c. treated
   d. improved

3. A good *remedy* for the dwindling resources problem is to reduce our dependence on nonrenewable fuels.
   a. decrease
   b. comparison
   c. poison
   d. solution

4. Our experience *suggests* that combustion ejects more noxious substances into the air than any other activity.
   a. indicates
   b. proves
   c. concludes
   d. states directly

5. Cold germs are *conveyed* in small drops of moisture ejected during sneezing and coughing.
   a. monitored
   b. detected
   c. carried
   d. connected

6. *Combustion* cannot take place in a vacuum.
   a. burning
   b. pollution
   c. combining
   d. destruction

7. Many of the elements contained in cigarette smoke are *noxious*.
   a. common
   b. helpful
   c. hazardous
   d. compounds

B. Mark the following statements T if they are true or F if they are false.

_____ 1. An activity that is on the decline is increasing in frequency.

_____ 2. Something that threatens you is a danger to you.

_____ 3. A fossil is a group of plants and animals in their usual environment.

_____ 4. Bonding is the process of burning.

_____ 5. To alter something is to put it in a high place.

_____ 6. To eject something is to keep it alive.

_____ 7. A particle is smaller than a mass.

_____ 8. Air is one of the agents that sustain human life.

_____ 9. In a photovoltaic cell silicon interacts with the sun's rays.

_____ 10. Bad colds can lead to more serious diseases.

C. Choose the correct lettered response to complete each numbered statement.

1. Particles conveyed by the air are _____.
   a. extinct
   b. airborne
   c. ejected
   d. sustained

2. What is the environmental _____ of continuing water pollution?
   a. impact
   b. moisture
   c. particle
   d. bonding

3. Another word for the environment a specific group of plants and animals occupy is the _____.
   a. mass
   b. issue
   c. impact
   d. ecosystem

4. Devising ways to decrease gasoline consumption is a _____ to today's designers.
   a. combustion
   b. challenge

c. remedy

d. fossil

5. Increased cigarette smoking in a population leads to increased _____.
   a. moisture
   b. bonding
   c. particles
   d. mortality

6. The _____ of fuel consumption is one that causes a lot of controversy.
   a. challenge
   b. remedy
   c. issue
   d. combustion

7. A group of animals that once lived on earth but no longer does is _____.
   a. sustained
   b. contaminated
   c. altered
   d. extinct

8. Many doctors believe that eating too many fats is _____.
   a. extinct
   b. conveyed
   c. suggested
   d. hazardous

9. The impact of the wind tunnel research data has been _____.
   a. contaminated
   b. hazardous
   c. considerable
   d. noxious

10. Only one species of shark can _____ in lake water.
    a. survive
    b. sustain
    c. eject
    d. interact

11. Solar energy will probably soon be _____ as an important alternate power source.
    a. conveyed
    b. threatened
    c. contaminated
    d. classified

12. A blood clot is a _____ of solidified blood.
    a. remedy
    b. mass
    c. moisture
    d. mortality

Scanning for Specific Information

As you learned in Lesson Five (and from your familiarity with Landsat's multi-spectral scanner), scanning involves looking for specific information in a text you know contains it. This skill requires practice. Remember, the multispectral scanner looked over the entire surface of the earth so that individual details could be studied. The following exercise will help you build your scanning ability.

Scanning for Specific Information

EXERCISE

D. Read the questions first. Then quickly scan the reading on pages 140-142 to find the answers. Copy short answers from the text in the space provided.

1. What are the names of three fossil fuels? _____
   _____

2. What does H_2SO_4 stand for? _____

3. What does HNO_3 stand for? _____

4. Where has acid rain been a problem? _____
   _____

5. What is the pH of uncontaminated rain? _____

6. What is one of the lowest rainstorm pHs ever recorded? _____

7. Where was it recorded? _____

8. What percentage of Scandinavian lakes have no fish? _____

Understanding Vocabulary from Word Parts

Roots

Study the following word parts. The examples with asterisks have been used in this text.

alter, altr (related to change or "other")
alter*
alternate*
alteration

aqua, aque, aqui (related to water)
aquatic*
aquarium

eco (related to interaction of a community)
ecology
ecosystem*
economics

solu, solv, solut (related to weakening or loosening)
dissolve
soluble
solve

mor, mort (related to death)
mortality*

Understanding Vocabulary from Word Parts: *Roots*

EXERCISE

E. In an English dictionary look up the following words. Copy a short definition for each. Make a mental note of how the root relates to the rest of the word.

1. alternating current _____

_____

2. aqueous humor _____

_____

3. aquiculture _____

_____

4. aquifer _____

_____

5. mortal _____

_____

6. solute _____

_____

7. solvent _____

_____

Two scientists study the effect of acid water on fish.
U.S. Fish & Wildlife Service

Reading Selection

Acid Rain: Its Effect on the Aquatic Ecosystem

aquatic: related to water in lakes, rivers, and streams; sometimes to seawater

ponds: small lakes

Although there is a lot of controversy about solutions to the problem of acid rain, many observers say that it will become a worldwide **challenge** to aquatic **ecosystems** if nothing is done soon. Acid rain is currently polluting lakes and ponds throughout the northeastern part of Canada and the United States as well as in Scandinavia and Germany. Many of these acidic lakes have lost their ability **to sustain** life—particularly fish life. **In spite of** the controversy over **remedies**, everyone agrees that if we don't reduce the acid rain, we will have no more freshwater fish. **1**

freshwater: lake and stream water, not salt water

Fossil Fuel Combustion Wastes

En route: on the way

How does acid rain occur? Research indicates that much of the acid rain is caused by the burning of organic, or fossil, fuels, such as coal, oil, and gas. The combustion of this fuel **ejects** gases, sulfur dioxide (SO_2), and nitrogen oxides (NO_x)* into the atmosphere. These pollutants can be **conveyed** hundreds and even thousands of kilometers by large air **masses**. En route, many of the **airborne** oxide **particles** fall back to earth. Through the process of chemical **bond-** **2**

*Where x equals a large but unknown number.

dew: morning or evening moisture that forms with temperature changes

ing, the oxides can be transformed by a rainstorm, falling snow, or even dew, into sulfuric acids (H_2SO_4) and nitric acids (HNO_3). These acids are **noxious** to plant and animal life. **Furthermore,** the oxides can also **interact** chemically with the **moisture** in the flowing air mass to form acid rain or snow.

There are now some atmospheric surveillance stations where rain acidity can be monitored. **Uncontaminated** rain has a pH of 5.6 (pH is a measure of acidity, with 0 being very acid, 7 being neutral, and 14 very alkaline. On this scale lemon juice, an acid, would have a pH of 2.2, and baking soda, an alkali, would have an 8.5 pH). Rain can be **classified** as acidic, and **thus hazardous,** if its pH falls below 5. **Nevertheless,** the average pH of a rainstorm in the northeastern United States is 4.0. Moreover, Wheeling, West Virginia, reported a pH of 1.4, one of the lowest ever recorded.

3

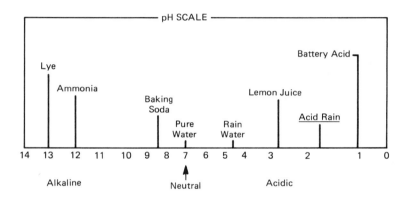

Impact of Acid Rain on Fish Life

Acid rain **leads to** fish **mortality.** Many species of fish **cannot survive** in aquatic environments where the pH is below 5.0. If the water is too acid, the gill systems of many kinds of fish can be damaged. **Besides,** the acid **alters** the blood chemistry of all fish. **As a result,** the fish population in an acidic environment decreases or becomes **extinct.** Approximately 20 percent of the lakes in Scandinavia are without fish. In the Adirondack mountains of the American state of New York, there are no fish in more than 200 lakes. **Moreover,** in Nova Scotia the entire salmon industry may be **threatened** by the decrease of salmon in rivers and streams. The impact is also **considerable** in the waters of Ontario and Quebec, where fish populations are **on the decline.**

4

What potential remedies exist for the acid rain **issue?** The experts disagree. Some say new environmental laws should be

enacted: passed and
put to work

smokestacks: large
tubes that release
smoke from factories

enacted to control the emission of pollutants in the atmosphere. Some say that if we had known how serious acid rain was, we would have planned better to prevent it. Nevertheless, all agree that if the consumption of fossil fuel were reduced, we would have less of a problem. Another possibility is that special scrubbers could be installed in smokestacks to remove a good portion of the pollutants 5 before they get into the atmosphere. Other ideas even include breeding more tolerant fish. And research **suggests** that spreading lime into lakes may be effective in reducing acidity. **In conclusion,** it is clear that if we truly want to reduce the impact of acid rain, a combination of remedies and international cooperation must be explored. It is a sad fact that acid rain probably could have been avoided if we had known what we know now.

Comprehension

EXERCISE

F. Mark the following statements T if they are true or F if they are false.

_____ 1. Everyone agrees on the correct remedy for the acid rain problem.

_____ 2. Acid rain threatens the aquatic ecosystem.

_____ 3. Acid rain is a unique problem of the oceans.

_____ 4. All acid rain results from the combustion of organic fuels.

_____ 5. Sulfur dioxide and nitrogen oxides are pollutants.

_____ 6. The oxides can be carried by the air.

_____ 7. The pollutants remain forever airborne.

_____ 8. Airborne moisture can convert the oxides into dangerous acids.

_____ 9. H_2SO_4 and HNO_3 are harmful to plants and animals.

_____ 10. pH is a measure of relative acidity.

_____ 11. Lemon juice is acid only under certain conditions.

_____ 12. When rain has a low pH, it is hazardous.

_____ 13. Acid in lake water inhibits the respiration of all kinds of fish.

_____ 14. All Scandinavian lakes are populated by extinct fish.

_____ 15. The salmon industry has been aided by the oxides.

_____ 16. Decreasing the fossil fuel consumption rate would have an impact on the acid rain problem.

_____ 17. Special scrubbers are currently in wide use.

EXERCISE

G. Choose the correct lettered response to define each numbered word.

1. salmon (¶ 4)
   a. an alkali
   b. a fish
2. atmosphere (¶ 2)
   a. air
   b. atoms
3. baking soda (¶ 3)
   a. an acid
   b. an alkali
4. scrubbers (¶ 5)
   a. tolerant workers
   b. pollution removers
5. emission (¶ 5)
   a. reduction
   b. ejection
6. good (¶ 5)
   a. large
   b. harmless
7. lime (¶ 5)
   a. an acid
   b. an alkali
8. tolerant (¶ 5)
   a. understanding
   b. hardy

Drawing Conclusions

EXERCISE

H. Draw conclusions from the reading. Choose the correct lettered response to complete each numbered statement.

1. Fossil fuels are made of _____.
   a. the bodies of long-dead plants and animals
   b. solar energy
2. The lower the pH, _____.
   a. the more acid the material
   b. the more alkaline the material

3. The controversy about this issue _____.
   a. mainly involves the remedies
   b. mainly involves the fish industry

4. The problem of acid rain needs international cooperation _____.
   a. because the oxides can be conveyed from one country to another
   b. because Americans won't buy salmon from polluted waters

5. Salmon fishing is _____.
   a. an important industry in Nova Scotia
   b. more important now than it was the past

6. The author suggests that _____.
   a. we are close to a solution of this problem
   b. this problem is severe and needs immediate attention

COMPREHENSION SKILL INDEX

If Clauses

Understanding the meaning of sentences using the word *if* is a key to understanding the author's ideas. The verbs contained in such sentences indicate whether the author is describing a general fact, predicting what will happen in the future (under certain conditions), or speculating on what might have been, had certain conditions existed in the past. This structure is heavily used in scientific and technical writing because it is the language of hypothesis and theory.

examples:

1. *If* clauses in present tense sentences express statements of fact and belief.

   If sugar and water are mixed, they *go* into solution.

   People in poor nations *can be fed* if amaranth is widely cultivated and distributed.

2. *If* clauses in sentences with *will* express predictions about the future.

   If the text contains a detailed coverage of the acid rain problem, I *will buy* it.

   I *will be able* to understand it if it is not too difficult.

3. *If* clauses in sentences with *would* express the probable outcome of a set of conditions that do not exist now.

   If industry installed scrubbers, part of the problem *would be remedied.*

   Finding a solution *would be easier* if nations cooperated with each other.
   If Latin were more widely studied, understanding new words *would be easier.*

   You *would be frightened* if a shark were near.

4. *If* clauses in sentences with *would have, could have, might have,* or *should have* express what could have happened in the past under certain conditions which did not exist.

> If we had known the effect of releasing pollutants into the air, we *could have* (*would have, might have,* and so on) *planned* better.

> The patient *could have avoided* true eye surgery if he had been in a large city with a hospital equipped to do laser surgery.

If Clauses

EXERCISE

I. Choose an explanation from the list to explain the meaning of the following sentences taken from the reading.

A   prediction about the future
B   general statement of fact or belief
C   probable outcome of a set of conditions that do not exist now
D   probable outcome of a set of conditions that did not exist in the past

_____ 1. If we don't reduce the acid rain, we will have no more freshwater fish.

_____ 2. Rain can be classified as hazardous if its pH falls below 5.

_____ 3. Acid rain will become a worldwide challenge to aquatic ecosystems if nothing is done.

_____ 4. If the consumption of fossil fuels were reduced, we would have less of a problem.

_____ 5. Some say that if we had known how serious acid rain was, we would have planned better to prevent it.

_____ 6. If we truly want to reduce the impact of acid rain, a combination of remedies and international cooperation will have to be explored.

_____ 7. If the water is too acid, the gill systems of many kinds of fish can be damaged.

_____ 8. It is a sad fact that acid rain probably could have been avoided if we had known what we know now.

Review the meaning of the modals.

ability: can, could
She knew she could perform laser surgery as well as any other doctor.

advisability: ought to, ought to have; should, should have
He should consider amaranth a good subject for study.

expectation: should, should have
An earthquake should occur within the next two years.

necessity: have to, had to; must, must have
The rule is that you must wear eye protection when working with acids in this lab.

possibility: may, may have; might, might have; could, could have
Scientists might identify the cancer-inhibiting factor in shark blood.

probability: must, must have
He must know that most sharks don't attack humans.

Modal Auxiliaries: Active and Passive

EXERCISE

J. Indicate whether the following sentences containing modals express ability, advisability, expectation, necessity, possibility, or probability. Some sentences have two possible answers. They are marked with an asterisk.

_____ 1. You must study in order to learn.

_____ 2. He should be here by nine o'clock.*

_____ 3. The acid rain problem may be the most serious environmental issue of the century.

_____ 4. If he had seen the shark, he could have gotten out of the water.*

_____ 5. Solar energy may be the energy source of the future.

_____ 6. We might have chosen laser surgery, if we had known about it.

_____ 7. Developing nations ought to be conducting research in amaranth hybridization.

_____ 8. Scientists may have found the solution to our growing energy needs.

_____ 9. Fossil records suggest that early humans must have been shorter than present-day humans.

_____ 10. We could not have foreseen the acid rain problem.

Passive Modals

Review the passive construction in Lesson Three.
Note that the passive form of the modal auxiliaries is constructed as follows.

modal + form of verb *to be* + past participle

example: Sunlight can be converted into electrical energy.

As you know, in a passive sentence the subject is the receiver of the verb's action.

subject modal form of verb to be past participle

examples: Sharks should be studied by cancer researchers.

subject modal to be past participle

This fact must have been understood at the beginning.

A fish fossilized in shale.

American Museum of Natural History

Storm clouds can carry airborne contaminants to faraway water systems, causing acid rain.

National Oceanic and Atmospheric Administration.

Passive Modals

EXERCISE

K. Underline the subject of the following sentences from the reading. Then indicate whether the modal expression indicates ability, advisability, expectation, necessity, possibility, or probability. Some sentences express more than one of these.

_____ 1. These pollutants can be conveyed hundreds and even thousands of kilometers by large air masses.

_____ 2. Through the process of chemical bonding, the oxides can be transformed by a rainstorm, falling snow, or even dew, into sulfuric acids and nitric acids.

_____ 3. There are now some atmospheric surveillance stations where rain acidity can be monitored.

_____ 4. Rain can be classified as acidic, and thus hazardous, if its pH falls below 5.

_____ 5. Moreover, in Nova Scotia the entire salmon industry may be threatened by the decrease of salmon in rivers and streams.

_____ 6. Some say that new environmental laws should be enacted to control the emission of pollutants into the atmosphere.

_____ 7. Another possibility is that special scrubbers could be installed in smokestacks to remove a good portion of the pollutants before they get into the atmosphere.

_____ 8. In conclusion, it is clear that if we truly want to reduce the impact of acid rain, a combination of remedies and international cooperation must be explored.

Vocabulary Review

EXERCISE

L. Many of the words used in the reading selection were vocabulary words from earlier lessons. Match each word in column a with its meaning in column b.

a	b
1. currently	to show
2. to reduce	surroundings
3. to indicate	organ of respiration
4. surveillance	now; at present
5. to monitor	possible
6. scale	to extend
7. environment	producing offspring
8. gill	to put in place for use
9. potential	to watch and record
10. consumption	watching carefully
11. to install	to decrease
12. breeding	use
13. to spread	reference standard

The Space Shuttle: A Combination of Aviation, Rocketry, and Satellite Technology

Two astronauts perform a simulated test mission on the flight deck of the orbiter.

Subtechnical Vocabulary

overhaul (noun)

complete inspection to discover problems, usually of a machine

Overhaul of this aircraft requires six hours of careful work.

maintenance (noun)

work necessary to keep something in working condition

Even the most aerodynamically advanced car will get poor gas mileage if it doesn't receive the proper **maintenance**.

personnel (noun)

people with the necessary training to complete a certain job

Laboratory **personnel** should all be familiar with fire safety rules.

crew (noun)

team of personnel on a large moving vehicle, such as a ship or a plane

The **crew** on all commercial flights has been trained to function in all sorts of emergencies.

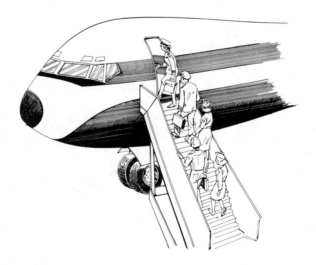

controls (noun)

instruments used to pilot a plane or operate machinery

During an airplane flight the pilot usually operates the **controls**.

deck (noun)

area on a ship or a plane where the crew works; comparable to one story of a building; for example, upper deck, lower deck, and so on

The food preparation area on some of the jumbo jets is below the passenger **deck.**

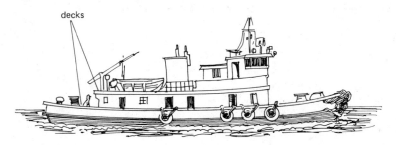

quarters (noun)

area where personnel go when they have finished their work

Most commercial airplanes are so fast that it is not necessary to provide the crew with sleeping **quarters.**

cargo (noun)

material transported by a moving vehicle

When the truck had the accident, its entire **cargo** fell onto the road.

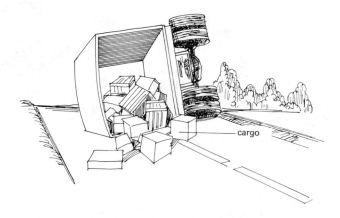

storage (noun)

the placement of objects in such a place that they will remain safe and in good condition for later use

The main function of the refrigerator is food **storage.**

retrieval (noun)

> the action of taking back an object that has been in another place
>
> Once something is thrown into the sea, the ocean currents make **retrieval** very difficult.

hatch (noun)

> door on the deck of a ship or plane leading to the storage area
>
> After the cargo was put in storage, the **hatch** remained closed for the entire trip.

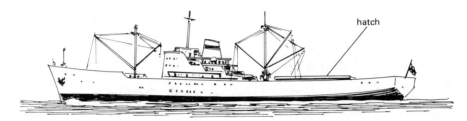

hatch

maneuvers (noun)

> purposeful movements made by a plane or a ship either in order to enable the crew to observe something or in order to go in a particular direction
>
> Landsat's daily **maneuvers** provide over 130 countries with information they want.

payload (noun)

> personnel, equipment, and cargo on a spacecraft needed for the spacecraft to perform its work
>
> Landsat's **payload** is the multispectral scanner.

task (noun)

> specific job to be done
>
> Her **task** was to interpret pixels.

configuration (noun)

> form of a manufactured product; physical arrangement of a designed product; for example, an airplane
>
> Many passenger planes are manufactured in two **configurations**: regular length (standard) and extended length (stretch).

facilities (noun)

> places specially designed to provide specific services
>
> Generally, elementary schools do not have laboratory **facilities**.

goal (noun)

> main purpose
>
> The **goal** of the recent shark research is to determine if the cancer-inhibiting factor in shark blood has potential use in human cancer prevention.

to propel (verb)

> to cause to move forward with a lot of force
>
> Engines **propel** jet aircraft.

to glide (verb)

> to fly without fuel, making use of wind, air currents, and an aerodynamically designed craft
>
> The smaller, propeller-driven aircraft had better ability **to glide** than jet planes do.

to tow (verb)

> to pull or carry from one place to another
>
> When a car has no gasoline, it is often necessary **to tow** it to the service station.

to display (verb)

> to show; to make visible
>
> The results of some experiments **can be displayed** on a graph, making it unnecessary to read long narratives and descriptions.

to pressurize (verb)

> to keep the interior of an aircraft or spacecraft at a normal air pressure
>
> The passenger cabin of all commercial aircraft **is pressurized** for the comfort and safety of the passengers.

to initiate (verb)

> to start
>
> The launching of Sputnik in 1958 **initiated** the space age.

to accomplish (verb)

    to perform to completion; to complete successfully

    He **accomplished** his task in half the time he thought it would take.

to simulate (verb)

    to duplicate by imitation; to pretend to be the same as something else

    Wind tunnels **simulate** the conditions a vehicle will encounter when it moves through the air.

optical (adjective)

    related to sight

    Microscopes and telescopes are **optical** instruments.

Vocabulary of Ideas

to carry out (phrasal verb)

    to accomplish; to perform

    The crew **carried out** the orders and instructions of the captain.

faced by

    encountered by; subjected to

    One of the conditions **faced by** the astronauts who went to the moon was decreased gravity.

Thought Connectors

i.e.

    Recently there has been a decrease in mortality from the major diseases, **i.e.**, stroke, cancer, and heart attacks.

hence

    The plant is very hardy, **hence** its name, amaranth, which means "unfading" in Greek.

Vocabulary Exercises

A. Complete the following sentences with words from the list.

faced by	maneuvers	simulate	goal	maintenance
optical	overhaul	facilities	deck	pressurize

1. It is not necessary to _____ a vehicle unless it will carry passengers and crew.

2. After 10,000 kilometers most cars require a complete _____.

3. The _____ of the wind tunnel studies is to help designers understand aerodynamics.

4. Most buses do not provide passengers with bathroom _____.

5. Seismologists want to _____ the movement along faults so that they can better understand what happens when stress builds up.

6. The controls to an airplane can be found on the flight _____.

7. It is the task of the captain to initiate _____.

8. A difficulty _____ space travelers is an oxygen-poor atmosphere.

9. An _____ illusion is a distortion of perception causing the viewer to see something that does not exist.

10. The human body requires protein for _____ and repair.

B. Choose the correct lettered response to complete each numbered statement.

1. Even if a plane uses up all its fuel, it can sometimes _____ to the ground.
   a. tow
   b. glide
   c. propel
   d. carry out

2. The personnel, equipment, and cargo involved in the tasks to be carried out by a spacecraft are its _____.
   a. facilities
   b. controls
   c. crew
   d. payload

3. Images from the multispectral scanner are _____ on a screen so that observers can identify land features.
   a. initiated
   b. displayed
   c. accomplished
   d. propelled

4. Scientists predict that laser arterial plaque reduction surgery will be _____ on humans in the near future.
   a. pressurized
   b. simulated

c. initiated

d. displayed

5. In order to get to the cargo, the crew must pass through a _____.

    a. maneuvers

    b. hatch

    c. configuration

    d. storage

6. Many books are available in hard-cover and soft-cover _____.

    a. configurations

    b. maneuvers

    c. facilities

    d. goals

7. When a glider airplane lands, it must be _____ to a storage area.

    a. pressurized

    b. glided

    c. simulated

    d. towed

8. Most people feel good once a difficult _____ is accomplished.

    a. overhaul

    b. task

    c. payload

    d. hatch

9. The crew's _____ were small and uncomfortable.

    a. quarters

    b. controls

    c. cargo

    d. personnel

10. Some airplanes are passenger planes, and some are _____ planes.

    a. optical

    b. crew

    c. payload

    d. cargo

11. The efficient _____ of cargo is an important requirement in commercial aviation.

    a. overhaul

    b. storage

    c. configuration

    d. goal

12. The _____ of satellites is often more difficult for ground personnel than launching them is.

    a. storage

    b. retrieval

c. task
d. deck

13. The most important person on an airplane is the one who operates the _____.
    a. controls
    b. maintenance
    c. payload
    d. hatch

14. It is hoped that the hybridization of amaranth will be _____ soon.
    a. displayed
    b. simulated
    c. accomplished
    d. towed

15. After lime is put in lakes with high acidity, pH studies are _____ to see if the water has become more alkaline.
    a. simulated
    b. pressurized
    c. displayed
    d. carried out

16. When a person sneezes, droplets of moisture are _____ through the air.
    a. propelled
    b. initiated
    c. pressurized
    d. carried out

17. Hospital _____ often have to work through the night.
    a. personnel
    b. storage
    c. cargo
    d. retrieval

18. The _____ on the ship is trained in the most modern methods of bad-weather sailing.
    a. overhaul
    b. crew
    c. configuration
    d. deck

COMPREHENSION SKILL INDEX

Understanding Vocabulary from Word Parts

Roots

Study the following word parts. The examples have all been used in Lessons One to Nine.

main, man (related to the hand)
maintenance

maneuvers
manufacture

habit (related to places lived in)
inhabit

jet, ject (related to throwing)
eject
jettison

loc (related to specific places)
local
locate

Understanding Vocabulary from Word Parts:
Roots

EXERCISE

C. Look up the following words in an English dictionary. Copy a short definition for each one. Make a mental note of the relationship of the root word part to the meaning of the word as a whole.

1. manual _____

2. manipulate _____

3. manuscript _____

4. habitat _____

5. habitable _____

6. inhabitant _____

7. inject _____

8. projectile _____

9. locus _____

10. locality _____

COMPREHENSION SKILL INDEX

Understanding Vocabulary from Word Parts

Suffixes

Knowing some common English suffixes will enable you to increase your vocabulary. Unlike prefixes, which are a clue to the meaning of a particular word, the suffixes we will study in this text generally change the part of speech of the base word, for instance, from a verb to a noun.

It is important to be aware that there are two classes of suffixes in English. Class 1 suffixes are the common verb endings, plural endings, the endings that make adjectives comparative or superlative, and the endings that are used to indicate possession.

examples: class 1 suffixes

-s, -es:	simulate**s**, accomplish**es**
-d, -ed:	pressurize**d**, propell**ed**
-ing:	tow**ing**
-s, -es:	control**s**, hatch**es**
-er, -est:	wild**er**, hardi**est**
's:	Mary**'s**

Class 2 suffixes are the suffixes we will study in this text. They enable you to recognize and therefore understand the same word in a variety of possible roles; that is, as nouns, verbs, adjectives, adverbs, and so on.

examples: words ending in class 2 suffixes

Noun	Verb	Adjective	Adverb
specula*tion*	specul*ate*	specul*ative*	specul*atively*
depend*ence*	depend	depend*able*	dependab*ly*

Note that words with class 2 suffixes often freely attach class 1 suffixes.

examples: speculations, speculating

Do not assume, however, that it is necessary to add a suffix to change the part of speech. Hundreds of English words are used with no change in form as both nouns and verbs. These examples are taken from this text.

Noun	Verb
break	to break
breed	to breed
display	to display
function	to function
poison	to poison
process	to process

example: There is a **display** of data on the screen. This page **displays** seven examples of words used both as nouns and verbs.

Suffixes

EXERCISE

D. In the space provided, indicate whether the boldface suffix is class 1 or class 2.

_____ 1. glid**es**

_____ 2. retrie**val**

_____ 3. initiat**ing**

_____ 4. initia**tive**

_____ 5. configur**ation**

_____ 6. orbit**al**

_____ 7. emis**sion**

_____ 8. consist**ing**

_____ 9. Landsat**'s**

_____ 10. manipula**tive**

COMPREHENSION SKILL INDEX

Understanding Vocabulary from Word Parts

Suffixes (continued)

Here and in the next few lessons, we will study class 2 suffixes. The value of this study is in making you familiar enough with the common suffixes so that once you know a word in one form, you will understand it in any form in which you may find it.

Study the following list. You will notice that sometimes the suffix causes a spelling change in the base word. Do not be concerned. Your goal is recognition and comprehension, not spelling.

Suffixes That Make Nouns from Verbs

-age
to store   storage

-al
to survive   survival

-ance, -ancy, -ence
to maintain   maintenance
to convey   conveyance

-ation, -cation, -ition, -sion, -ssion, -tion
to conserve   conservation
to identify   identification
to compose   composition

to conclude	conclusion
to permit	permission
to correct	correction

-y

to injure	injury
to discover	discovery

-ice

to serve	service

-ment

to equip	equipment

-t

to extend	extent

-ture, -ure

to proceed	procedure
to mix	mixture

A satellite view of the space shuttle's orbiter shows the cargo bay section.

NASA

The Space Shuttle: A Combination of Aviation, Rocketry, and Satellite Technology

The liftoff of the first space shuttle occurred in early 1981. Since then the National Aeronautics and Space Administration (NASA) has completed several test missions and is planning to launch more than seventy additional missions by 1987.   **1**

The space shuttle looks like a delta-winged aircraft and is about the size of a DC-9 passenger plane. On either side of this main craft are two solid fuel boosters which **propel** the shuttle into an orbital path around the earth. In a typical mission the main engines and solid fuel boosters fire together at the time of liftoff. Then, at burnout, which occurs when the craft reaches an altitude of approximately 45 kilometers, the boosters are jettisoned and later recovered   **2** on earth. The main craft, sometimes called the Orbiter, then orbits the earth at speeds of up to 27,400 kilometers per hour. When the shuttle completes a mission, it reenters the earth's atmosphere, **glides** to the ground, and lands on a runway the way an airplane does. It **is** then **towed** to ground facilities for **overhaul** and **maintenance**, and prepared for reuse. The space shuttle is the world's first reusable spacecraft.

burnout: stopping of combustion

jettisoned: thrown off

The major **goal** of the space shuttle is to carry a **payload** of **personnel** and equipment into orbit, **to initiate** and **accomplish** various **tasks,** and then to return to earth. This is made possible by the unique and comfortable **configuration** of the craft. The flight **crew** travels in the crew module, a cabin containing the **controls** in the forward section of the spacecraft. The flight **deck** in the upper   **3** portion of this command module contains the living **quarters,** consisting of a galley, bathroom **facilities,** and sleeping accommodations. Aft of the flight deck is the **cargo** bay section, which is the major payload **storage** section. This 18-meter-long storage area carries all scientific equipment for observing space objects and for conducting scientific experiments.

forward: front

galley: kitchen
aft: behind
bay: compartment

An important feature of the cargo bay section is the "Canada," the main manipulating arm for **carrying out** satellite placement and **retrieval maneuvers.** Another name for this arm is RMS, which stands for remote manipulator system. It is mounted behind the cabin area on one side of the payload bay. This key   **4** instrument was a gift from Canada, **hence** its name. The astronauts can enter the cargo bay through an airlock and **hatch** located in the lower deck. All sections inhabited by the crew **are pressurized** to an atmospheric pressure that **simulates** sea level.

mounted: placed securely

airlock: place where air pressure can be regulated

An important task of the space shuttle will be to launch a space telescope and place it in an orbit about 500 kilometers above the earth. This orbiting telescope will be the largest **optical** instrument in space. It is about 13 meters long and 4 meters in diameter, and it weighs about 10,000 kilograms. With the space telescope astronomers will be able to study other space objects, **i.e.** stars, comets, planets, and other galaxies. The telescope will also make it possible to identify celestial objects seven times more distant than   5
those that can be seen with earth-based telescopes. Instruments aboard the satellite will take pictures and measure the distance between space objects as well as the distance of the objects from earth. The pictures will also aid in the determination of the space objects' composition. All this information will be converted into electronic signals, or pulses, and beamed to earth. On earth astronomers will use computers to reconstruct the images and **display** them on television screens.

The space telescope will be superior to earth-based telescopes for another reason. The main problems **faced by** users of telescopes are the clouds, smog, and bad weather that can prevent accurate viewing of objects in space. In contrast, in space there is an absence   6
of weather and therefore no such interference. The space telescope will be able to provide astronomers with a clear view of the universe every day of the year.

comet: space object with a tail; observed only when it is near the sun

galaxy: large group of planets and space objects associated with each other

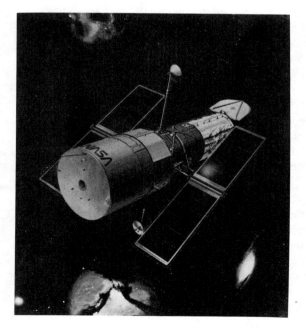

A drawing shows the space telescope to be launched into orbit in the mid-1980s by the space shuttle.

Perkin-Elmer Corporation

Comprehension

E. Find *one* word or a number in the text to complete the following statements.

1. The first space shuttle was launched in the winter or spring of

   _____.

2. NASA's current plan is to put many more _____ into space in the next several years.

3. The main craft is approximately the same _____ as a DC-9.

4. After burnout the boosters are _____ from a height of 45 kilometers.

5. The speed of the main craft's orbit reaches _____ kilometers per hour.

6. Upon a mission's completion, the main craft _____ the same way as an airplane.

7. After the landing the _____ is pulled to the overhaul and maintenance area.

8. This spaceship is the first to be _____.

9. The main purpose of the space shuttle is to put crew and equipment into orbit in order to perform certain tasks and then to _____ safely.

10. The form and design of the Orbiter are both _____ and comfortable.

11. Aboard the Orbiter the controls are found in the _____ module.

12. The living quarters provide cooking facilities, bathrooms, and accommodations for

    _____.

13. The _____ area is behind the command module.

14. The observation equipment is stored in the _____ bay.

15. The RMS was given to the United States by _____.

16. So that the crew will be comfortable, the air _____ is the same as it would be on earth.

17. The space shuttle will _____ the supertelescope.

18. A telescope is an _____ device.

19. The telescope will enable scientists to _____ remote objects in space.

20. The tasks of the space telescope involve distance measurements and

_____ determinations.

21. The information received by the instruments aboard the orbiting satellite will then be

transformed into electronic pulses and _____ to earth.

22. These images will then be shown on _____ screens.

23. Three problems that limit the success of telescopes are bad weather, smog, and

_____.

24. These problems do not exist in space because space lacks _____.

Vocabulary in Context

EXERCISE

F. Choose the correct lettered response to define each numbered word.

1. liftoff (¶ 1)
   a. launch
   b. removal

2. mission (¶ 1)
   a. purposeful trip
   b. religious center

3. to fire (¶ 2)
   a. to stop working
   b. to start combustion

4. runway (¶ 2)
   a. escaping place
   b. landing place

5. boosters (¶ 2)
   a. rockets
   b. orbits

6. module (¶ 3)
   a. model
   b. cabin

7. stands for (¶ 4)
   a. replaces
   b. means

8. key (¶ 4)
   a. airlock opener
   b. very important

9. sea level (¶ 4)
   a. on earth
   b. salt water
10. telescope (¶ 5)
    a. instrument for observation
    b. television screen
11. celestial (¶ 5)
    a. space
    b. beautiful

COMPREHENSION SKILL INDEX

Spatial Relations

Although you have known these words since early in your English studies, any confusion about their meanings can completely ruin your comprehension of a reading passage. These words are key in understanding technical writing, since in this sort of writing there are frequent descriptions of machinery. You must understand the meaning of words that express spatial relations if you want to get a mental picture of these descriptions.

Review the following terms for spatial relations. If there are some you are not sure of, look them up in a bilingual dictionary. Pay particular attention to the third group, the prepositions and adverbs.

Nouns	Adjectives
front/back	horizontal/vertical/diagonal
rear	perpendicular/parallel
left/right	upper/lower
top/bottom	inner/outer
interior/exterior	forward/aft
center/side	
middle/edge	
corner	
north/south	
east/west	
inside/outside	

Prepositions, Adverbs, and Other Expressions

aboard	beneath	near	through
above	beside	off	throughout

across	between	on	to
against	beyond	onto	toward
along	by	on either side of	under
alongside	down	on top of	underneath
around	in	out	up
at	in front of	outside	upon
behind	inside	over	with
below	into	surrounded by	within

Spatial Relations

EXERCISE

G. Look at the following diagram of the space shuttle. Then circle the word that correctly describes the spatial relationship.

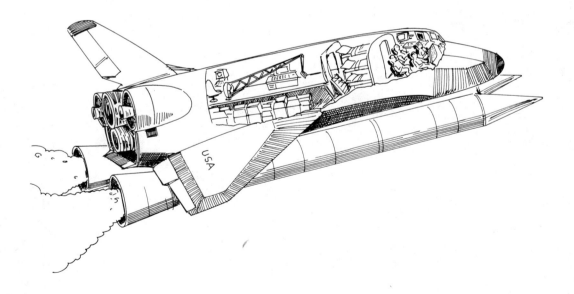

(1)
We can see the crew *around/aboard* the space shuttle. The command module is in
(2)   (3)
the *forward/aft* section of the Orbiter. *Surrounded by/Above* the captain's head is a
(4)   (5)
screen. There are probably some images *inside/on* it. *In front of/Alongside of* the captain
(6)
are the controls. This flight deck occupies the *lower/upper* portion of the crew's cabin.
(7)
The solid fuel boosters are mounted *on top of/on either side of* the Orbiter at the time of
(8)
liftoff. Later, at burnout, these are jettisoned to be recovered *below/above* on the ground.
(9)   (10)
Behind/Below the crew's living quarters in the *lower-upper* part of the Orbiter is the cargo
(11)   (12)
bay. *Beside/Inside* this storage area is the RMS, which is mounted *on top of/on one side*
(13)
of the bay. In order to get to the cargo bay, the crew must pass *through/between* the

hatch.

A photo taken from the flight deck shows the testing of a remote
manipulator system in the cargo bay.
NASA

Maglev: A New Generation in Railroad Technology

The Maglev moves down its guideway.

Subtechnical Vocabulary

fatality (noun)

> death caused by an unusual or unexpected situation
>
> The crash resulted in many **fatalities.**

generation (noun)

> phase in the evolution of a machine
>
> The first **generation** automobiles were very different from those of today.

prototype (noun)

> the first example of a new machine, usually manufactured for testing
>
> One of the most important steps in the development of a new car is the testing of a **prototype** in a wind tunnel.

acronym (noun)

> new word formed by combining the first letters (sometimes the first syllables) of other words
>
> Laser is an **acronym** for light amplification by stimulated emission of radiation.

propulsion (noun)

> process, force, or action of propelling or driving; forward movement
>
> Jet **propulsion** and rocket **propulsion** are very powerful.

suspension (noun)

> process, force, or action of holding, hanging, or supporting an object above the floor or ground
>
> A cloud of air pollution holds harmful particles in **suspension** in the lower atmosphere.

coil (noun)

> a series of connected concentric spirals
>
> A **coil** can be shaped like a cylinder or like a cone.

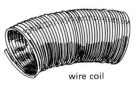

wire coil

braking (noun)

> process of slowing down; reducing speed

> **Braking** is less efficient on a wet surface.

burst (noun)

> sharp emission or release of energy or substance

> In laser arterial plaque reduction, short **bursts** of laser light are emitted into the artery through a fiber glass tube.

friction (noun)

> movement of one object against the surface of another

> **Friction** generates heat.

vibration (noun)

> sensation caused by movement

> A passing train often causes a lot of **vibration**.

breakdown (noun)

> mechanical malfunction which prevents operation

> The mechanic said the car's **breakdown** was caused by a broken gear.

breakdown

wear and tear (noun)

> damage caused by use

> Rough roads result in excessive **wear and tear** on tires.

moving part (noun)

> one mechanical component of a machine, for example, a gear; a component of a machine that can be separated from the rest of the machine

> Watches have many **moving parts**.

to race (verb)

>to move or operate very quickly
>
>A heart that **races** is sometimes a sign of thyrotoxicosis.

to float (verb)

>to remain suspended in the air or in water without sinking to the bottom or falling to the ground
>
>In spacecraft where gravity is reduced, the astronauts **float.**

to cradle (verb)

>to hold closely and securely, in somewhat the same way a person holds a baby
>
>The seats **are cradled** by the frame of the car.

to attract (verb)

>to pull toward some other object
>
>Sharks **are** often **attracted** to a particular area by the presence of blood.

to repel (verb)

>to cause to move away; opposite of *to attract*
>
>Divers have been searching for a substance that **repels** sharks.

to diminish (verb)

>to reduce; to be reduced; to decrease
>
>Braking causes the car's speed **to diminish.**

to switch on (phrasal verb)

>to turn on, particularly electrical power or lights
>
>After the photovoltaic cell was installed, the power **was switched on.**

successive (adjective)

>sequential; following in order
>
>There are four **successive** bells to indicate the immediate departure of the train.

like (adjective)

>same; equal
>
>**Like** poles repel each other.

unlike (adjective)

>opposite; unequal

>Birds and fish are **unlike** in almost all respects.

conventional (adjective)

>ordinary; not technologically sophisticated

>A complication of **conventional** surgery is infection.

immediately (adverb)

>directly

>In this list of words the word **immediately** preceding *prototype* is *generation.*

Vocabulary of Ideas

virtually (adverb)

>almost; practically

>Scientists are **virtually** certain that there is a cancer-inhibiting agent in the blood of the shark.

in excess of

>more than

>There are **in excess of** three hundred species of sharks in the world's oceans.

on the cutting edge

>in the forefront of all those conducting or applying research; very advanced in technology

>The scientists at this university are **on the cutting edge** of cancer research.

with lightning speed

>extremely fast; figurative for "with the virtual speed of lightning"

>The jet plane raced down the runway **with lightning speed**.

to be referred to as

>to be called; to be known as

>Solar cells **are** often **referred to as** photovoltaic cells.

Vocabulary Exercises

A. Complete the following statements with words from the list.

referred   acronym   like   successive   attracts

virtually   moving parts   immediately breakdown   generation

1. Sugar _____ flies.

2. When he had _____ completed all the tasks, he learned that he would have to repeat all of them because of an error he made at the beginning.

3. _____ following a great buildup in stress an earthquake is likely to occur.

4. Two right gloves are _____ gloves.

5. The last three _____ missions of the space shuttle have been entirely successful.

6. It can take a lot of time to repair a _____ in telephone lines.

7. UNESCO is an _____ for the United Nations Educational, Social, and Cultural Organization.

8. Landsat is _____ to as an earth resources technology satellite.

9. Machines with too many _____ are more likely to break down.

10. The new _____ computers are much smaller than the early ones.

B. Choose the correct lettered response to complete each numbered statement.

1. Two things that are unequal or opposite are referred to as _____ things.
   a. like
   b. conventional
   c. unlike
   d. successive

2. Propeller airplanes are sometimes called _____ airplanes.
   a. like
   b. conventional
   c. floating
   d. unlike

3. If you put the like poles of two magnets near each other, they will _____ each other.
   a. diminish
   b. race

c. cradle

d. repel

4. An earthquake produces a lot of _____.
   a. generation
   b. suspension
   c. propulsion
   d. vibration

5. After years of _____, many moving parts have to be replaced.
   a. wear and tear
   b. braking
   c. propulsion
   d. breakdowns

6. If a wire _____ is straightened out, it is much longer than it appeared in spiral form.
   a. suspension
   b. acronym
   c. coil
   d. generation

7. Every day people in all kinds of vehicles—cars, buses, trains, and planes—

   _____ to their jobs.
   a. float
   b. race
   c. attract
   d. repel

8. Some earthquakes are so powerful they cause hundreds of thousands of

   _____.
   a. moving parts
   b. fatalities
   c. acronyms
   d. wear and tear

9. The personnel in this laboratory were responsible for the publication of

   _____ of one hundred articles reporting their research last year.
   a. with lightning speed
   b. the cutting edge
   c. in excess
   d. immediately

10. Wood and paper _____; iron and stones do not.
    a. race
    b. float
    c. attract
    d. cradle

11. At liftoff there is usually a huge _____ of smoke from the combustion of the fuel.
    a. suspension
    b. vibration
    c. fatality
    d. burst

12. _____ of new models are not for sale; they are used for testing only.
    a. Coils
    b. Breakdowns
    c. Acronyms
    d. Prototypes

13. When returning to earth, the space shuttle's two solid fuel rocket boosters are kept safe through _____ from a parachute.
    a. suspension
    b. propulsion
    c. breakdown
    d. friction

14. Landsat moves _____ over the entire surface of the earth.
    a. on the cutting edge
    b. with lightning speed
    c. immediately
    d. in excess

15. The Japanese have been for some time _____ of new technology.
    a. on the cutting edge
    b. with lightning speed
    c. in excess
    d. successive

16. Many doctors feel that reducing the amount of fat in the diet will _____ the rate of production of arterial plaque.
    a. switch on
    b. race
    c. repel
    d. diminish

17. The _____ of an airplane is accomplished by several means; in the air the flaps are manipulated, and on the ground the engines are reversed.
    a. moving part
    b. braking
    c. wear and tear
    d. suspension

18. After the earthquake power was not _____ again for more than a week.
    a. switched on
    b. with lightning speed
    c. referred to
    d. diminished

19. The heart is _____ inside the chest.
    a. raced
    b. switched on
    c. diminished
    d. cradled

20. Initially _____ of the space shuttle is carried out by the solid fuel rocket boosters.
    a. propulsion
    b. suspension
    c. braking
    d. wear and tear

COMPREHENSION SKILL INDEX

Understanding Vocabulary from Word Parts

Suffixes

Study the following nouns formed from adjectives by use of the indicated suffixes.

-ance, -ancy, -ence, ency

Adjective	Noun
abundant	abundance
dependent	dependency
evident	evidence
pregnant	pregnancy
significant	significance

-ity

Adjective	Noun
absurd	absurdity
acid	acidity
active	activity
alkaline	alkalinity
capable	capability

conventional	conventionality
fatal	fatality
normal	normality
polar	polarity
possible	possibility
potential	potentiality
probable	probability
reliable	reliability
responsible	responsibility
visible	visibility

-ness

Adjective	Noun
fierce	fierceness
remote	remoteness
small	smallness

The Bullet Train races down the track.
Japanese National Railways

Maglev: A New Generation in Railroad Technology

The Japanese have one of the most advanced mass railroad systems in the world. The Shinkansen, **referred to** as the Bullet Train, covers thousands of kilometers of tracks at speeds **in excess of** 200 kilometers per hour. Each day the more than 270 bullet-nosed trains convey 340,000 passengers throughout Japan. Since the Japanese system went into service in 1964, the trains have carried more than 1.8 billion travelers without an injury or a **fatality**. The well-maintained system is not only safe and fast, but it is not petroleum dependent.

1

The Japanese National Railways made a huge investment in time, money, and technical personnel in building the Shinkansen. Now, as always, **on the cutting edge**, they are working on developing the next **generation** of high-speed supertrains.

2

Technical specialists working at the Japanese National Railways have been experimenting with a **prototype** magnetic levitation train. The maglev (an **acronym** for magnetic levitation) will actually **race** along a guideway at almost 500 kilometers per hour, **floating** on a magnetic field. The maglev will operate on the basic principles of electromagnetism.

3

The train depends on magnetism for **propulsion, suspension, and braking.** Specialized sets of magnetic **coils** are built into the body framework of the train. Other sets of magnetic coils are installed in the bottom and sides of a U-shaped guideway that **cradles** the train. When electric power is **switched on,** the coils on the train and in the guideway produce a magnetic field with north and south poles. The magnetic forces between the coils on the train and the coils in the guideway can be made **to attract** or **repel** each other by changing their polarity. The train is propelled by magnetic attraction between the magnets aboard the train and those on the guideway. As the **successive** and rapid **bursts** of magnetism move from coil to coil **with lightning speed,** the train accelerates after them, resulting in the forward movement of the train. In summary, then, the magnetic coils on the train are attracted by the opposing polarity of the guideway coils **immediately** ahead of them.

4

Magnetism is also used to lift the train off the guideway to reduce **friction, diminishing wear and tear** where the train meets the guideway. The special coils aboard the train and on the guideway repel each other, making the train float. This repulsion force is so strong that it can lift a moving 10,000-kilogram train 10 centimeters off the guideway. The braking action is accomplished by

5

changing the polarity of the train coils relative to those of the guide-way coils, reversing their relationship from one of attraction between two **unlike** poles to one of repulsion between two **like** poles.

Japanese National Railway System engineers believe the new maglev trains will be an improvement over the Shinkansen. Not only will the maglev be faster than the Bullet, it will be more comfortable and more reliable as well. Since the maglev rides on a magnetic wave, it has a low noise level and a diminished **vibration** level. This is an important consideration for the people living in neighboring areas, 6 particularly in a country with such high population density. Low maintenance is another advantage of the maglev train because of the fact that the maglev has no **moving** motor **parts** or steel wheels as **conventional** trains do. This factor **virtually** eliminates guideway wear and tear and prevents costly **breakdowns**. In addition, much less time will be spent on equipment inspection, track repair, and parts replacement.

The Japanese are still conducting test runs of the new pro-totype maglev train. But they expect to have several of them running 7 by the end of the decade.

Comprehension

EXERCISE

C. Mark the following statements T if they are true or F if they are false.

_____ 1. Another name for the Shinkansen is the Bullet Train.

_____ 2. The Shinkansen is not a fast train.

_____ 3. The Shinkansen has 270 noses.

_____ 4. No one has died in an accident on the Shinkansen since it went into service in 1964.

_____ 5. The Shinkansen is not as safe as petroleum-powered trains.

_____ 6. The Japanese are working on a new train.

_____ 7. This new train is not yet in service.

_____ 8. The Shinkansen is faster than the maglev.

_____ 9. The maglev does not run on a conventional track.

_____ 10. Two sets of magnetic coils are responsible for the movement of the maglev.

_____ 11. Lightning powers the maglev.

A close-up view shows the construction of the maglev's guideway.
Japanese National Railways

_____ 12. Magnetism not only propels the maglev, but it also suspends it above the guideway.

_____ 13. Suspension is important for wear-and-tear reduction.

_____ 14. The maglev floats.

_____ 15. The maglev train uses conventional brakes.

_____ 16. The maglev does not vibrate as much as the Shinkansen.

_____ 17. Maintenance on the maglev will be less costly than maintenance on the Bullet Train.

_____ 18. The maglev train causes almost no guideway wear and tear.

Vocabulary in Context

EXERCISE

D. Choose the correct lettered response to define each numbered word.

1. mass (¶ 1)
   a. relating to a large number of people
   b. unknown

2. covers (¶ 1)
   a. passes over
   b. hides

3. investment (¶ 2)
   a. expenditure
   b. clothing

4. levitation (¶ 3)
   a. horizontal
   b. floating

5. principles (¶ 3)
   a. firsts
   b. laws

6. framework (¶ 4)
   a. wheels
   b. support

7. guideway (¶ 4)
   a. direction
   b. specialized runway

8. accelerates (¶ 4)
   a. speeds
   b. slows

9. after (¶ 4)
   a. in search of
   b. later than

10. reversing (¶ 5)
    a. remaining
    b. changing

11. consideration (¶ 6)
    a. factor
    b. impossibility

12. neighboring (¶ 6)
    a. remote
    b. nearby

COMPREHENSION SKILL INDEX

Preposed Modifying Clusters

It is common in scientific and technical descriptive writing to combine two or more words and use them as an adjective to modify a noun. When these adjectives precede the noun, they are usually hyphenated. In this text compound adjectives that precede the noun are called preposed modifiers.

examples: blue-green algae

self-sustaining plants

eight-meter-long shark

> well-known theory
>
> low-cost maintenance
>
> delta-winged aircraft
>
> sharklike fish

As with the noun compounds, an easy way to understand phrases made up of compound adjectives and the nouns they modify is to look immediately at the noun. Then ask yourself, "What is the author saying about this (*insert the noun*)?" "What kind of (*insert the noun*) is this?"

One of the compound adjective types listed above is used very frequently in scientific and technical writing because it permits us to name and describe new things or previously unknown facts.

example: delta-winged aircraft (made up of an adjective, or a noun functioning as an adjective, plus a past participle made from a noun)

Preposed Modifying Clusters

EXERCISE

E. Follow the model.

delta-winged aircraft ⟶
an aircraft that is delta-winged

1. delta-winged aircraft _____

   _____

2. U-shaped guideway _____

   _____

3. bullet-nosed train _____

   _____

4. long-legged insect _____

   _____

5. self-supporting laboratory _____

   _____

6. self-powered rocket _____

   _____

7. self-generating power cell _____

_____

8. yellow-orange light _____

_____

9. one-meter-deep fault _____

_____

10. high-level fever _____

_____

11. high-speed supertrain _____

_____

12. eyelike organ _____

_____

13. tracklike guideway _____

_____

14. petroleum-dependent system _____

_____

15. well-maintained road _____

_____

COMPREHENSION SKILL INDEX

Reduced Adverb Clauses Introduced by *-ing* Words

As you read more and more complex materials, you will encounter longer sentences that express more than one idea, with the separate ideas related to each other in some way. One way of relating ideas is through an adverb clause. Remember that adverbs modify verbs, adjectives, or other adverbs.

examples: Because radon builds up in ground water immediately before earthquakes, seismologists speculate that radon levels could serve as an early warning system. (Answers the question, Why do seismologists speculate that radon levels could serve as an early warning system?)

When the cancer-inhibiting agent in shark blood is identified, it can be used in human cancer prevention. (Answers the question, When can this agent be used in human cancer prevention?)

Unless amaranth can be hybridized to produce a more reliable seed, it is unlikely that its cultivation will be economically successful. (Answers the question, Under what circumstances will amaranth cultivation be economically successful?)

Adverb clauses generally answer the questions when, why, how, and under what circumstances? These clauses are often introduced by a word that indicates these ideas, such as *after, before, when, if, until, because, unless,* and so on.

In many sentences expressing these same idea relationships, however, the word is left out and the adverb clause simply becomes a phrase that modifies the verb in the main clause of the sentence. These adverb phrases will answer the questions when, why, how, and under what circumstances. These phrases are referred to as reduced adverb phrases.

examples: when?

Leaving the airlock section, the astronauts discovered a breakdown in the hatch to the cargo bay. (This is a reduced form of: When they were leaving the airlock section, the astronauts discovered a breakdown in the hatch to the cargo bay.

why?

Containing all the parts that are known to reduce fuel efficiency (side mirrors, for example), this prototype car was not even subjected to wind tunnel studies. (This is a reduced form of: Because it contains all the parts that are known to reduce fuel efficiency (side mirrors, for example), this prototype car was not even subjected to wind tunnel studies.)

how?

The engineer was able to bring the train to a complete stop, reversing the polarity of the magnetic coils. (This is a reduced form of: The engineer was able to bring the train to a complete stop by reversing the polarity of the magnetic coils.)

Remember that the *-ing* words that introduce these phrases do not function as gerunds (nouns), participles (adjectives), or progressives (verbs).

Reduced Adverb Clauses Introduced by -ing *Words*

EXERCISE

F. In the following sentences indicate whether the italicized *-ing* word introduces an adverb phrase or functions as a noun, adjective, or progressive verb.

_____ 1. Professor Smith was *developing* a new technique of laser surgery.

_____ 2. *Developing* new techniques of laser surgery is the most important goal of the surgeons at this hospital.

_____ 3. *Developing* a new technique of laser surgery, Professor Smith accidentally discovered that lasers could be used to clean conventional surgical instruments.

_____ 4. *Developing* nations with food supply problems will be able to increase their food production when amaranth becomes commercially available.

_____ 5. While the shark was *swimming* near the diver, the diver thought she should remain behind the old ship.

_____ 6. *Swimming* near the shark, the diver thought it would be a good idea to stay out of sight behind the ship.

_____ 7. *Swimming* near a shark is not the best idea in the world.

_____ 8. A *swimming* diver is more attractive to a shark than a still diver is.

Vocabulary

BOOK 1

Alphabetical listing of Subtechnical Vocabulary and Vocabulary of Ideas with reference to the lesson the word comes from

about	5	braking	10
(to) accomplish	9	breakdown	10
(to) account for	1	breakthrough	6
acronym	10	(to) breed	4
adaptable	4	(to) build up	2
(in) addition	8	burst	10
agent	5	cargo	9
(to) aid	5	(to) carry out	9
airborne	8	cell	6
(to) alert	5	challenge	8
(to) allow	6	(to) check	1
(to) alter	8	(to) classify	8
alternate	6	close to	4
antenna	6	clot	1
artery	2	coil	10
(to) associate	3	combustion	8
(to) attack	5	(to) come along	4
(to) attract	10	(to) come from	3
bare	7	(in) comparison	1
base	6	compound	4
beam	2	(to) conclude	5
besides	8	(in) conclusion	8
blight	7	(to) conduct	6
bonding	8	configuration	9

consequently	7	(in) excess of	10
considerable	8	(to) expand	7
(to) consist	6	(to) extend	4
consumption	6	extinct	8
(to) contaminate	8	faced by	9
controls	9	facilities	9
conventional	10	fatality	10
(to) convert	6	feasibility	4
(to) convey	8	feature	7
coronary	2	(to) feed on	5
count	2	ferocious	5
(to) cradle	10	fiber glass	2
crew	9	field	5
crop	4	firstly	7
(to) cross	4	(to) float	10
(to) cultivate	4	force	1
currently	6	(to) forecast	3
(to) cut down on	1	for this reason	7
(on the) cutting edge	10	fossil	8
cycle	5	frequency	5
damage	3	friction	10
(on the) decline	8	fuel	1
decay	3	full-size	1
deck	9	furthermore	8
deep-sea	2	gill	5
delicate	2	(to) generate	6
(to) depend	6	generation	10
deposit	2	(to) glide	9
(to) detach	2	goal	9
(to) develop	3	grain	4
(to) devise	3	ground	3
diameter	6	hardy	4
diet	4	(to) harvest	4
(to) diminish	10	(to) hatch	9
(to) display	9	hazardous	8
(to) distribute	6	hereditary	4
(to) dwindle	6	(to) identify	7
earthquake	3	image	7
ecosystem	8	immediately	10
(to) eject	8	impact	8
(to) emerge	7	(to) indicate	1
(to) emit	2	(to) inhibit	5
(to) encounter	1	(to) initiate	9
environment	4	inner	2
(to) equip	7	(to) insert	2
essential	4	(to) install	1

(to) interact	8	propulsion	10
(to) involve	1	prototype	10
issue	8	quarters	9
(to be) known to	5	(to) race	10
(to) launch	6	ratio	1
(to) lead to	8	reading	3
level	3	(to) record	3
(with) lightning speed	10	(to) reduce	1
like	10	(to be) referred to as	10
maintenance	9	(to) refine	6
maneuvers	9	remedy	8
marginal	4	(to) remove	2
mass	8	(to) renew	6
(to) mature	4	(to) repel	10
(to) miss	4	(to) replace	5
model	1	(to) report	3
moisture	8	resistance	1
(to) monitor	3	resource	6
moreover	8	(as a) result	8
mortality	8	(to) result from	2
moving part	10	retractable	1
network	3	retrieval	9
nevertheless	8	(to) rid	5
noxious	8	row	5
(a) number of	5	scale	3
obstruction	2	(to) scan	7
offspring	4	sequential	7
optical	9	set	5
orbit	6	(to) set up	3
over	3	shade	7
(to) overcome	1	(to) shine	2
(to) overhaul	9	(to be) short of	4
(to) overlap	7	(to) shut off	2
particle	8	signal	7
pattern	7	signs	2
payload	9	(to) simulate	9
personnel	9	slight	3
pest	4	soil	7
(to) pick up	5	some examples	7
pit	5	somewhat	7
plankton	5	(to) sort out	7
potential	7	species	4
(to) precede	3	spectrum	7
(to) pressurize	9	(to) speculate	3
prey	5	(in) spite of	7
(to) propel	9	(to) standardize	7

storage	9	thus	8
streamlined	1	(to) tow	9
stress	3	trait	4
(to) stretch	6	(to) transform	6
stroke	2	tube	2
subject to	1	uniform	4
successive	10	unique	7
(to) suffer from	2	unlike	10
sufficient	6	up to	5
(to) suggest	8	(to) use up	6
(to) supply	2	vacuum	1
surface	3	vibration	10
surgery	2	virtually	10
surveillance	7	waste	6
(to) survive	8	wear and tear	10
suspension	10	(to) wear out	5
(to) sustain	8	wide range of	4
(to) switch on	10	width	1
(to) take a look at	5	wild	4
(to) take (+ time)	4	wing	6
task	9	wire	6
therefore	7	yield	4
(to) threaten	8		

Glossary

The following high-frequency words, in the context used in the text, were chosen for translation as a quick reference device.

ENGLISH	SPANISH	PORTUGUESE
accuracy	exactitud	exatidão
(to) add	añadir	adicionar
(in) advance	por anticipado	antecipadamente
adverse	desfavorable	adverso
aft	a popa	à pôpa; de pôpa
aircraft	aeronave	aeronave
airlock	antecámara de compresión	cãmera de compressão
(to) align	alinearse	alinhar
amount	cantidad	quantidade
angle; at right angles	ángulo; en ángulo recto	ângulo; em ângulo reto
antibody	anticuerpo	anticorpo
around	alrededor de	em volta, em tôrno
(to) arrange	arreglar	arranjar, arrumar
as a whole	generalmente	em conjunto
ash	cenizas	cinzas
(to) assist	ayudar	ajudar
assistant	ayudante	assistente
(to) assume control	tomar control	tomar contrôle
(to) attach	atar	atar, ligar
attachment	unión	ligação, junção
(to) attend	asistir	assistir
attendant	asistente; ayudante	assistente
available	disponible	aproveitável
average	promedio; término medio	média; médio
(to) avoid	evitar	evitar
aware	consciente	ciente
axis	eje	eixo
back	de atrás	de trás
backache	dolor de espalda	dor nas costas; dor lumbar
back and forth	de atrás para adelante	para trás e para frente
backwards	hacia atrás	para trás
baked	asado al horno	assado, cozido no forno
baking soda	bicarbonato de soda	bicarbonato de sódio
barn	granero	celciro, palheiro
barn owl	lechuza bodeguera	coruja-de-igreja
bay	compartimiento	compartimento
beak	pico	bico
beating	golpeando	batendo
(to) become	llegar a ser	tornar-se, vir a ser
behavior	comportimiento	comportamento
behind	detrás de	atrás, detrás
belief	creencia	crença
(to) believe	creer	crer
bell	campana	campainha
below	abajo; debajo	abaixo, debaixo
belt	cinturón	cinto

ENGLISH	SPANISH	PORTUGUESE
(the) bends	aeroembolia; parálisis de los buzos	mal-dos-caixoẽs; mal-dos-mergulhadores
(to) bend	doblar	dobrar
beneath	abajo	abaixo
berry	fruta pequeña como mora, frambuesa, etc.	qualquer fruto do tipo morango, amora, framboesa, etc.
beside	cerca de	ao lado de
beyond	más allá	além
billion	mil millones	bilhão, bilião
bird	pájaro	ave, passaro
birth	nacimiento; parto	nascimento
blade	hoja	fôlha, lâmina
(to) blame	culpar	culpar, responsibilizar
bleeding	flujo de sangre	sangrando
blindness	ceguera	cegueira
blood	sangre	sangue
(to) blow	soplar	soprar
boardlike	como una tabla	como uma tábua
body (of water)	extensión (de agua)	extensão de água
body	cuerpo	corpo
(to) boil	hervir	ferver
boiler	calorífero	caldeira
boldface	negrillas	negrito
bond	grado de afinidad	ligação
bonded	pegado	ligado
bone	hueso	osso
booster	sección propulsadora	foguete reforçador
boring	aburrido	chato, aborrecido
(to be) born	nacer	nascer
bottom	fondo	fundo
box	caja	caixa
brain	cerebro	cérebro
brakes	frenos	freios
(to) break	romper	quebrar, romper
(to) break free	desatarse	libertar-se; desunir-se
(to) breathe	respirar	respirar
bridge	puente	ponte
bright	brillante	brilhante
broad (selection)	amplio	amplo, extenso, largo
broken	quebrado; roto	quebrado; roto
bubble	burbuja	bôlha, borbulha
(to) build	construir; hacer	construir, fazer
building	edificio	edifício
bulb	bombilla	bulbo; lâmpada
burn	quemadura	queimadura
(to) burrow	amadrigarse	fazer toca; escavar
business	comercio; negocio	negócio, comêrcio
cap (polar ice cap)	capa	calota glacial do poío
capable	capaz	capaz
care	cuidado; atención	atenção; cuidado
careful	cuidadoso	cuidadoso
(to) carry	llevar; conducir	carregar, levar
(to) catch	capturar; agarrar	apanhar; agarrar
century	siglo	século
chain	cadena	cadeia
change	cambio	mudança; cámbio
(to) channel	acanalar	acanalar; canalizar
charcoal	carbón de leña	carvão vegetal
checkerboard	tablero (de damas)	tabuleiro (de damas)
chest	pecho	peito
childbirth	parto	parto
chin	mentón	queixo
(to) choose	escoger	escolher

ENGLISH	SPANISH	PORTUGUESE
(to) churn	revolver; agitar	bater; agitar
claw	garra	garra
clean	limpio	limpo
(to) climb	ascender	ascender
close	cerca	perto
cloth	tela	tecido, pano
clothing	ropa	roupa
cloud	nube	nuvem
clue	indicio	indício
coal	carbón de piedra	carvão
(to) coin a word	crear una palabra nueva	inventar uma palavra nova
concern	preocupación	preocupação (interêsse)
conference	consulta	conferência
container	envase; caja	recipiente
conveyance	transporte	transporte
cooking	cocina	arte culinária, cozinha
cooky	galletita	bolacha, biscoito
(to) cool	enfriarse	arrefecer
core	parte central	âmago, centro
corn	maíz	milho, grão
corner	esquina; rincón	esquinha; canto
cost effective	que rinde más beneficio por el coste	a maneira mais eficaz por o custo
costly	caro	custoso
cotton	algodón	algodão
(to) cough	toser	tossir
crack	grieta	greta
cracker	galleta	bolacha
craft	nave; vehículo	nave espacial, nave do espaço
crash	choque	colisão, choque
crawling	andando a cuatro patas	rastejar
(to) cross out	tachar	riscar
cruising speed	velocidad de viaje	velocidade de cruzeiro
crushing	aplastante	esmagante
crust	corteza	crosta
cup	taza	taça
(to) cure	remediar	curar
cure	remedio	cura, remédio
daily	diario	diário
damp	húmedo	úmido
danger	peligro	perigo
dangerous	peligroso	perigoso
dark	oscuro	escuro
(to) date back to	tener su comienzo en	datar de
dead	muerto	morto
(to) deaden	amortiguar	amortecer
(to) deal with	encargarse de	lidar com; ocupar-se com
death	muerte	morte
deathly	cadavérico	mortal
debt	deuda	dívida
(to) decline	disminuir(se)	declinar
(to) decrease	disminuirse	diminuir(-se)
deep	profundo	profundo
degree	grado	grav
(to) deliver	entregar; transmitir	entregar
departure	salida	partida, saída
depressed	hundido; aplanado	deprimido
(to) design	diseñar	designar
(to) destroy	destruir	destruir
(to) detect	percibir; advertir	descobrir
device	aparato	invenção; aparelho
(to) devote	dedicarse	dedicar-se a
dew	rocío	orvalho
dexterity	destreza	destreza

ENGLISH	SPANISH	PORTUGUESE
(to) diffuse	difundir	difundir
dirt	suciedad	sujeira
disagreement	desacuerdo	desacôrdo
(to) discourage	desanimar; disuadir	desencorajar
disease	enfermedad	doença
(to) display	exhibir; mostrar	exibir; mostrar
disturbance	alteración; desarreglo	perturbação; distúrbio
diver	buceador	mergulhar
(to) divide	partir	dividir
diving	buceo	mergulho
dizziness	vértigo	vertigem
donkey	burro	asno
(to) dope	suavizar	aplicar
drag	resistencia al avance	arrastamento; resistência do ar
(to) draw (conclusions)	concluir	concluir
drop	gota	gôta
drought	sequía	sêca
drug	droga	droga
(to) dry	secar	secar
dust	polvo	poeira
ear	oreja	orelha
earth	tierra	terra
earthly	terrestre	terrestre
earth-based	apegado a la tierra	com base na terra
earth-bound	con rumbo a la tierra	com destino a terra
effective	eficaz	eficaz
effort	esfuerzo	esfôrço
empty	vacío	vazio
(to) enact	promulgar	decretar; promulgar
(to) enclose	encerrar; incluir	encerrar
(to) endure	aguantar	suportar, agüentar
(to) engage in	participar (en)	ocupar-se (em); envolver-se (em)
engine	máquina; motor	máquina; motor
enterprise	empresa	emprêsa
entrepreneur	empresario	empreiteiro, empreendador
exposed	expuesto	exposto
extent	grado	grau
fact	hecho	fato
(to) fail	fracasar; dejar de funcionar	falhar; falir
fair-skinned	blanco	tez clara; branco
familiar	conocido	bem conhecido
(to) fasten	fijar; atar	prender; segurar
fats	grasas	gorduras
fault	falla	falta, defeito
feather	pluma	pena, pluma
(to) feed	alimentar; alimentarse (de)	alimentar(-se)
female	hembra	fêmea
fierce	feroz	feroz
fiery	flameante	flamejante, ardente
fight	pelea; lucha	luta
finding	hallazgo	achado; descubrimento
finesse	delicadeza	finura, sutileza
(to) fit	caber; encajar (en)	caber, conformar
(to) fix	reparar	arrumar, consertar
fixed	fijo	fixo
flame	llama	chama
flap	guardafango; alerón	aba, borda
flight	vuelo	vôo
(to) flip	soltar	dar um piparote; saltar
flounder	lenguado	linguado
flour	harina	(flor de) farina
flow	flujo; derrame; corriente	fluxo, corrente
flue	humero; tubo de caldera	fumeiro

ENGLISH	SPANISH	PORTUGUESE
footnote	nota al pie de la página	nota ao pé da página
(to) forecast	pronosticar	prognosticar
forefront	vanguardia	vanguarda
forklift	elevador de carga	empilhadeira de forquilha; carroguindaste
foundry	fundición	fundição
framework	armazón	estrutura/armação
freshwater	(de) agua dulce	(de) agua doce
frightened	asustado	assustado
fuel-efficient	que requiere la menor cantidad de combustible	usar mais combustível
fuel-short	con escasez de combustible	com escassez de
furry	peludo	peludo
fuzzy	indistinto	impreciso
gain	ganancia; aumento	ganho; proveito
galley	cocina	galé
gauge	indicador	calibrador, indicador
(to) grind	moler; rechinar	moer; triturar
(to) grow teeth	echar dientes	endentecer; nascer os dentes
(to) guess	adivinar; suponer	adivinhar
(rain) gutter	canal de lluvia	goteira
(to) hang	colgar; suspender	pendurar; colgar
hardcover	libro encuadernado	livro encadernado
(to) harden	endurecer	endurecer
harm	daño	mal; dano
hawk	halcón	falcão
hay	heno	feno
head lamps	faroles	farois dianteiros
heat	calor	calor
heating	calefacción	aquecimento
hollow	hueco	ôco
hollow	cavidad; depresión	cavidade; vale
hood	cubierta	capuz; capô
hooked	ganchoso	munido de ganchos
(to) hunt	cazar	caçar
(to) hyphenate	escribir con guión	hifenizar
illness	enfermedad	doença
(to) injure	dañar; herir	ferir; injurar
injury	perjuicio; herida	ferimento; injúria
innards	interior; entrañas	tripas, entranhas
insulator	aislador	isolador
(to) interfere	impedir	interferir
investment	inversión	investimento
iron	hierro	ferro
italicized	en letra bastardilla	italicizado; grifado
(to) jettison	tirar	alijar carga (ao mar); tirar fora
joint	articulación	junta; ligação
junk food	comida sin valor nutritivo	comida sem valor nutritívo
keen	agudo	agudo, perspicaz
kidney stone	piedra nefrítica	cálculo renal
(to) kill	matar	matar
(to) label	calificar; apodar	rotular, etiquetar
(to) lace	entretejer	entrelaçar
land-based	con base en tierra	com base na terra
law	ley	lei; direito
layer	estrato	estrato, camada
(to) lead	conducir; dirigir	guiar, conduzir
lead	plomo	chumbo
leaf	hoja	fôlha
lens	lente	lente
lethal	letal; mortal	letal
license plate	placa, tablilla, patente	placa, chapa
lifespan	duración de vida	duração de vida

ENGLISH	SPANISH	PORTUGUESE
liftoff	despegue (de un cohete)	decolagem (de foguete)
light	claro	claro
light	liviano	leve
light	luz	luz
lightning	relámpago	relâmpago
likely	probable	provável
lime	cal	cal
limestone	caliza	calcário
link	vínculo	elo; argola
log	tronco; leña	tronco; livro de bordo
lonely	solitario; aislado	só; isolado
longstanding	de largos años	duradouro
lung	pulmón	pulmão
machinery	maquinaria	maquinaria
(to) make up for	compensar por	compensar
male	macho	macho
malnutrition	desnutrición	desnutrição
(to) master	conocer a fondo	dominar; tornar-se perito em
(to) match	hacer juego con	igualar; comparar
matter	asunto	assunto
matter	materia	matéria
(to) maximize	aumentar al máximo	maximizar
(to) measure	medir	medir
message	mensaje; comunicación	mensagem
midwife	partera	parteira
mileage	(millaje) kilometraje	milhagem (quilometragem)
(to) minimize	reducir al mínimo; subestimar	reduzir au mínimo
mirror	espejo	espelho
(to) mix	mezclar	misturar
morbidity	morbosidad	morbidez
mud flap	guardafango	páralama
nacelle	barquilla	nacele; barquinha
needle	aguja	agulha
non-prescription	(droga) no recetada	não-receitada
nozzle	boquilla	bico; bocal
nurse	enfermera	enfermeira
oat	avena	aveia
oil shale	esquisto petrolífero	xisto petrolífero
(to be) on the rise	estar subiendo	estar subindo
opening	abertura	abertura
outcome	resultado	resultado
outdoors	(al) aire libre	(ao) ar livre
outer	exterior; externo	exterior; externo
outlook	punto de vista	perspectiva; ponto de vista
(to) outperform	hacer mejor que	ultrapassar; exceder
outpost	puesto fronterizo	pôsto; posição avançado
(to) outweigh	pesar más; importar más que	exceder em pêso; ser mais importante
(to) outwork	trabajar más que	superar no trabalho
overactive	hiperactivo	demasiado ativo
overweight	obeso	obeso
owl	lechuza	coruja
ownership	posesión	propriedade; posse
pain	dolor	dôr
parachute	paracaídas	pára-quedas
passageway	pasadizo	passagem
patch	mancha	remendo; trecho
path	trayectoria	trajetória; trilha
pathway	conducto	caminho
(to) perch	posarse	empoleirar-se; pousar
(to) perform	ejecutar; desempeñar; ejercer	executar
petri dish	cápsula de Petri	o prato em que se faz culturas
phase	fase	fase
physician	médico	médico

ENGLISH	SPANISH	PORTUGUESE
(to) pick	escoger; recoger	escolher
pinwheel	girándula	girândola
pipe	cañaría; tubo	tubo, cano
(to) pipe	encañar	encanar; canalizar
placement	colocación	colocação
plains	llanuras	planicie
plate	plancha	placa
plentiful	abundante	abundante
(to) plug in	enchufar; conectar	fazer ligação; inserir
plywood	madera terciada	madeira compensada
point of view	punto de vista	ponto de vista
pointless	sin sentido	sem sentido
pointed	puntiagudo	pontudo
(to) point out	indicar; señaler	mostrar; chamar atenção para
poison	veneno	veneno
pollution	contaminación	poluição
pond	laguna	pequeno lago
poor	inferior; árido	inferior; infértil
poor	pobre	pobre
poorly	insatisfactoriamente	pobremente
(to) pose (a threat)	amenazar	propor uma ameaga; ameaçar
(to) pour	echar; fluir	fluir, correr
power	poder; energía	poder; energia
practitioner	médico	médico
pregnant	grávida	grávida
(to) prescribe	recetar	receitar
(to) pretend	aparentar	fingir; pretender
procedure	procedimiento	procedimento; processo
prone	propenso	propenso; inclinado
proof	prueba	prova
propeller	hélice	hélice
(to) propel	propulsar	propulsar
(to) provide	proveer	prover
(to) pump	bombear; circular	bombear
puzzle	misterio; problema; rompecabezas	quebra-cabeça; enigma
race horse	caballo corredor	cavalo de corridas
(to) radiate	emitir; irradiar	irradiar; radiar
rail	carril	carril
railroad	ferrocarril	ferrovia
railways	ferrocarril	linhas ferroviárias
rain gutter	canal de lluvia	goteira de chuva
rate	tasa; velocidad; porcentaje	taxa; velocidade; custo
rearward	hacia atrás	de retaguarda; traseiro
recall	memoria	lembrança
(to) recoup	recuperar	reembolsar
(to) redden	enrojecer(se)	avermelhar(-se)
red-hot	calentado al rojo	candente; aquecido ao rubro
reed	junco; caña	junco; cana
(to) refill	rellenar	reabastecer; reencher
(to) rely (on)	depender (de)	contar com
remorse	remordimiento	remorso
research	investigación	pesquisa
(to) retard	atrasar; retardar	atrasar; retardar
(to) return	regresar; volver; devolver	voltar; devolver
reusable	para uso repetido	para uso repetido
ring (of tree)	corte anular	camadas anuaís
risk	riesgo, peligro	risco, perigo
rocket	cohete	foguete
rodent	roedor	roedor
roof	techo	telhado
roost	percha	poleiro, pouso
rope	cuerda	corda
(to) rotate	girar; rotar	girar; rodar

ENGLISH	SPANISH	PORTUGUESE
rough	desigual; quebrado	impolido; irregular
rubber	caucho	borracha
ruff	collarín de plumas	gargantilha, coleira de penas
rules	reglas; leyes	regras; leis
running	funcionando	funcionando
run	prueba	prova
runway	pista	pista de decolagem
sailing	navegación	navegação
(to) save time	ahorrar tiempo	poupar tempo
sawdust	aserrín	serragem, serradura
(to) scatter	esparcir	espalhar
screen	pantalla	écran
scrubber	depurador	esfregador, purificador
scurvy	escurbuto	escorbuto
sea level	nivel del mar	nível do mar
(to) search (for)	buscar; anhelar	procurar, buscar
shallow	poco profundo	raso, pouco profundo
shark	tiburón	tubarão
(to) shift	mudar	mudar; trocar
(to) shorten	acortar; reducir	encurtar
shortness of breath	disnea	falta de fôlego
similar	semejante	semelhante
single	único; individual; singular	único; só; individual
(to) sink	sumergirse; descender	afundar, submergir
skill	habilidad	habilidade
(to) skim	ojear	deslizar à superfície
skull	cráneo	crânio
sleepiness	somnolencia	sonolência
slide rule	regla de cálculo	régua de cálculo
(to) slope	estar en declive	inclinar
(to) slow	retardar; disminuir la velocidad	retardar; diminuir a velocidade
smell	olor; olfato	odor; olfato
smog	humo mezclado con niebla	combinação de nevoeiro e fumaça
smoke	humo	fumaça; fumo
smokestack	chimenea; conducto de humo	chaminé
snout	hocico	focinho
(to) soar	remontarse	voar alto
(to) solve	solucionar	solucionar, resolver
somehow	de algún modo	de algum modo
sore	adolorido	sensível, dolorido
sought after	deseable	desejável, procurado
sound	sonido	som, sonido
source	fuente; origen	fonte; origem
spacecraft	astronave	astronave
speaker	conferenciante; altoparlante	orador, locutor; alto-falante
speed	velocidad	velocidade
speedometer	velocímetro	velocímetro
spelling	ortografía	ortografia
(to) spend time	pasar tiempo	passar tempo
(to) spill	derramar	derramar
spot	sitio	sítio, ponto
spot welding	soldadura de una área muy pequeña	soldadura de precisão
(to) spread	estirarse	estirar; estender
(to) spread out	difundirse	distender; difundir
spring	muelle	mola
square	cuadrado	quadrado
(to) stand for	representar; significar	representar; significar
(to) state	decir; formular	relatar; afirmar
steady	estable; continuo	estável; constante
steam	vapor	vapor
steel	acero	aço
(to) stick together	no separarse	conservar-se unidos
store	depósito; almacen	armázem

ENGLISH	SPANISH	PORTUGUESE
(to) store	almacenar	abastecer; armazenar
(to) straighten out	arreglar(se)	endireitar-se, pôr em ordem
stream	corriente	corrente
string	cuerda	cordão, corda
(to) struggle	luchar	lutar
subject	sujeto	sujeito
success	éxito	êxito
suitable	conveniente	conveniente
sunspot	mácula del sol	mancha solar
(to) superimpose	superponer	sobrepor
(to) support	apoyar; sostener; tolerar	apoiar; sustentar
(to) suppose	suponer	supor
(to) surface	emerger; volver a la superficie	emergir; vir à tona
(to) surmise	conjeturar	imaginar
(to) surpass	superar	superar
(to) surround	rodear; cercar	rodear; cercar
(to) suspect	sospechar	suspeitar
(to) sweep	barrer	varrer
sword	espada	espada
takeoff	despegue	decolagem
(to) take off	quitar(se)	levantar vôo; decolar
(to) take out	sacar; poner afuera	levar para fora, por fora
(to) take place	ocurrir; tener lugar	acontecer; ter lugar
talon	garra	garra
tanker	buque petrolero	(navio) petroleiro
team	equipo	equipe
tenfold	décuplo	décuplo
term	término	têrmo
test tube	tubo de ensayo	tubo de ensaio
threadlike	filiforme	filiforme
throat	garganta	garganta
(to) throw away	botar	deitar fora
tilt	inclinación	inclinação
topmost	predominante	o mais alto
treatment	tratamiento	tratamento
trench	fosa	fôsso
trial	ensayo	ensaio, prova
trim	adorno	alinho; apuro
trouble	inconveniencia	desgraça, dificuldade
underground	subterráneo	subsolo; subterrâneo
undersea	submarino	submarino
underside	parte de abajo	lado inferior
undigested	no digerido	indigerido
unfading	inmarchitable	imarcesível
(to) unscramble	desenrollar	pôr em ordem
unspoiled	no corrumpido	não estragado
vessel	vaso	vaso
warning	advertencia; alarma	aviso
wedge	cuña	cunha
weight	peso	pêso
(to) weld	soldar	soldar
well	pozo	poço
wheat	trigo	trigo
(to) whip	batir; agitar(se)	bater; chicotear
widespread	común; extendido	estendido; muito difundido
windmill	molino de viento	moinho de vento
windshield	parabrisas	párabrisa
wind tunnel	túnel aerodinámico	túnel aerodinâmico
wiring	canalización eléctrica	instalação elétrica; rêde elétrica
worldwide	global	mundial

ENGLISH	JAPANESE	ARABIC
abnormal	異常な	شاذّ
absorb	吸収する	يَمْتَصّ
to accelerate	加速する	يتسارع
accommodations	宿泊設備	وسائل الرّاحة
accumulation	集積	تراكُم
accuracy	正確さ	دقة ، صحة
acetylene	アセチレン	الأسيتيلينْ
acid	酸	حامض
acrylic	アクリルの	أكريلِيّ ، أكريليك
to activate	作動させる	يُنَشّطُ
adequate	十分な	كافٍ
administration	管理	إدارة
adverse	不利な	مُعادٍ ، معاكِسْ
aerodynamic	気体力学	إيرودينامي
aeronautics	航空学	علم الطيران
aerosol	エアゾール	الهباء الجوي ، دُخان
aerospace	大気および宇宙空間の	جو الأرض والفضاء الذي وراءه
agriculture	農業	زراعة
agrology	農業科学	علم التُربة
aircraft	航空機	منطاد أو طائرة
airlock	エアロック	قفل هوائي
air tanks	エアタンク	خزانات هواء
alarming	驚くべき	مُنذِر
alkali	アルカリ	قلوي
alternating current	交流	التيار المتردّد أو المتناوب
altitude	高度	الارتفاع
amaranth	アマランス	اللون الأرجواني الداكن
ambiguously	あいまいに	غامض
amino acid	アミノ酸	الحامض الأميني
amoeba	アメーバ	الأميبة
amplification	拡大	تكبير ، تضخيم
anachronism	時代錯誤	المفارقة التاريخية
analysis	分析	تحليل
anatomical	解剖（学上）の	تشريحي
anesthesia	麻酔	فقدان الحِس ، الخَدار
antibiotic	抗生物質	مضاد للجراثيم
antibodies	抗体	أجسام مضادة
anti-coagulative	抗凝固性の	مانع التخثُر
aquiculture	水生生物を養殖すること	تربية الحيوانات والنباتات المائية
aquifer	透水層	طبقة صخرية مائية
architect	建築家	المهندس المعماري
arsenic	ヒ素	زرنيخ
arthritis	関節炎	التهاب المفاصل
artificial	人工の	اصطناعي
asexually	無性の	لا تزاوجي
astronaut	宇宙飛行士	رائد الفضاء
astronomer	天文学者	الفلكي

ENGLISH	JAPANESE	ARABIC
asymptomatic	無症候性の	لا عَرَضي
atherosclerotic	アテローム性動脈硬化症の	مُتصلب الشرايين
atmosphere	空気、雰囲気	الغلاف الجوي
atom	原子	الذَّرة
to attach	つける	يربط ، يَضُمّ
automatic	自動的な	تلقائي ، أوتوماتيكي
autonomic	自律性の	ذاتي ، مُسْتَقل
aviation	飛行	الملاحة الجوية
bacteria	バクテリア	جراثيم ، بكتيريا
bacteriophage	バクテリオファージ（ウィルスの一種）	مُلْتهم الجراثيم
barometric	気圧の	البارومتري
barometric pressure	気圧上の	الضغط البارومتري
basking shark	ウバザメ	قرش مُسْتندِيء ، مُتَشَمِّس
beak	くちばし	مِنقار
beneficial	有益な	مفيد
biochemistry	生物化学	الكيمياء الحيوية
bioengineering	生物工学	الهندسة الحيوية
biology	生物学	علم الأحياء
biopsy	生体組織検査	استئصال نسيج من الجسد الحي ودراسته مجهرياً
bleeding	出血	نزيف
blindness	盲目	عمي
blood pressure	血圧	ضغط الدم
to boil	沸騰させる	يغلي
boldface	肉太の活字書体の一種	حرف أسود ، الطباعة بحرف أسود
bone	骨	عَظْم
boron	ホウ素	البورون : عنصر لافلزي يكون في البُورَق
botanist	植物学者	عالم النبات
brain	脳	دماغ ، ذكاء
to breathe	呼吸する	يتنفّس
cactus	サボテン	صبّار
caffeine	カフェイン	الكافيين ، البُنّ
calcium	カルシウム	الكلسيوم
calculation	計算	حساب
calorie	カロリー	سُعْر ، كالوري
cancer	癌	السرطان
capability	能力	قابلية ، قدرة
capacity	収容力	استيعاب
carbohydrate	炭水化物	الكربوهيدرات
carbon dioxide	二酸化炭素	ثاني أكسيد الكربون
carcinoma	癌種	سَرطان ، ورم سرطاني
category	範ちゅう	طبقة ، صِنْف
causation	原因になること	سَبَب
cavity	空洞	فجوة
centrifugal force	遠心力	القوة الطاردة من المركز
characteristic	特性、特徴	مُميِّز ، العدد البياني
charge	充電	يشْحَن
chemotherapy	化学療法	المعالجة (للأمراض) بالمواد الكيميائية
childbirth	出産	الولادة
chlorine	塩素	الكلور
cholesterol	コレステロール	الكولسْتيرول
chromium	クロム	الكروم
to churn	かき回す	يحرك بعنف ، يمخض اللبن
to circulate	循環する	يَنْشُر ، يدور
circumference	周囲	محيط الدائرة
circumstance	事情	ظرف ، حاله
to be classified	分類した	أن يكون مُصنَّف
clay	粘土	طين ، وحل
climate	気候	مُناخ
cloning	クローン	ارتجاف
clue	手がかり	مفتاح لحل لُغْز
coal	石炭	فحم نباتي
cobalt	コバルト	الكوبالت
coefficient	係数	المسمى (ر) ، المعامل

ENGLISH	JAPANESE	ARABIC
combination	配合	توحيد ، ضَمّ
comet	彗星	المُذَنّب
compartment	区画	قسم أو جزء مُسْتَقِلّ ، مقصورة في قطار
complication	複雑	تعقيد
component	構成要素	مُركّب
to compose	構成する	يُركّب
to concentrate	一点に集中する	يركز ، يكثّف
concentric	同心	متحد المركز
conception	概念	ادراك ، فهْم ، حمل
concrete	具体物	واقعي ، ملموس
to condense	凝縮する	يُكثّف
cone	円錐形の	مخروط
consequence	結果	نتيجة
conservation	保守	صيانة
constituent	構成している	تأسيسي
construction	建築	إنشاء ، تأسيس
to consume	尽きる	يستنفذ ، يستهلك
context	脈絡	سياق الكلام ، بيئة ، محيط
conversion	変換	تحويل
convincing	納得させる	مُقنِع
copper	銅	نحاس
core	しん	لُبّ ، جوْهر
corporate	団体の	مشترك
correlation	相関関係	علاقة مُتبادلة
cost-effective	費用効果の	إقتصادي
to counteract	反作用する	يُضاد ، يُبطِل
to create	造る	يخلُق ، يُبدِع
cross-fertilization	他家受精	الأخصاب التهجيني
crust	堅くなった表面	الجزء الخارجي من سطح الأرض ، الغلاف
crystal	水晶	بلّور ، شفاف
cure	治癒	علاج
cylinder	シリンダー	الاسطوانة
dam	ダム	سد ، خزّان
data	データ	معلومات ، حقائق ، بيانات
deaden	鈍くする	يميت ، يُهمِد
debilitated	衰弱した	جعله ضعيفاً ، مُضعَف
decompression	減圧	مزيل للضغط
deficiency	不足	نقص ، عجز
to deform	ゆがめる	يشوه
to demonstrate	明示する	يظهر بوضوح ، يتظاهر
density	密度	كثافة
dentistry	歯科医学	طب الأسنان
dependability	信頼性	إعتمادية
depressed	意気消沈した	مُقعّر السطح الأعلى ، منخفض ، حزين
depths	深さ	أعماق
determination	決定	التصميم ، ثبات في العزم
developing	発展途上にある	متطور ، نامي
device	装置	أداة ، وسيلة
dew	露	ندى
dexterity	機敏さ	براعة
diabetic	糖尿病の	ديابيتي : ذو علاقة بداء البول السكري
to diffuse	拡散する	ينشر (الضوء أو الحرارة)
diluted	薄められた	مخفف
dinosaur	恐竜	الدينصور
disaster	災難	كارثة
discouraged	落胆した	مُثبَّط الهِمّة
disease	病気	مَرض
disintegration	崩壊	انحلال
to dissolve	分解溶解する	يحل ، يُذيب
distortion	ゆがみ	تحريف ، تشويه
disturbance	乱れ	ازعاج ، اقلاق
dizziness	めまい	دوخة ، دوار
doctorate	博士号	درجة (أو لقب) الدكتوراه

ENGLISH	JAPANESE	ARABIC
dolomite	ドロマイト白雲石	الدولوميت
drought	乾燥	جفاف
dryness	乾燥	جفاف
eclipse	(太陽、月などの) 食	كسوف (الشمس) ، خسوف (القمر)
ecology	生態学	علم التبيؤ : فرع من علم الاحياء يدرس العلاقات بين الكائنات الحيّة وبيئتها
electrolyte	電解液(質)	الالكتروليت: المنحل بالكهرباء
electromagnet	電磁石	المغنطيس الكهربائي
electron	電子	الالكترون ، الكهيرب : شحنة كهربائية سالبة تشكل جزءاً من الذرة
element	要素	العنصر
to elevate	上げる	يقيم ، يرفع
emission	放出	اطلاق
endocrine	内分泌腺	هرموني
energy	エネルギー	طاقة
engineering	工学	هندسة
enormity	大罪	قباحة ، ضخامة
enterprise	企業	مؤسسة تجارية ، مشروع
entrepreneur	事業者	الملتزم ، المقاول
enzyme	酵素	خميرة ، أنزيمة
equator	赤道	خط الاستواء
ethics	倫理	أخلاق ، علم الأخلاق
etiology	原因	علم أسباب الأمراض
evaporation	蒸発する	تبخير
evolution	進化	تطور ، نشوء
to excrete	排せつする	يُفرز (العرق)
expectancy	予期	توقع
experiment	実験	اختبار ، تجربة
to exploit	開発する	يستخدم ، يستغل
exploration	探査	استكشاف
explosion	爆発	انفجار
eyesight	視力	بَصَر
fair-skinned	白色の肌の	بشرة فاتحة
farmlands	農地	مزرعة أو أرض صالحة للزراعة
fatal	命にかかわる	قدري ، مميت
to fertilize	受精する	يُلقِح ، يُسَمِّد
fever	熱	حمّى
fiber	繊維	نسيج ، خيط أو شيء كالخيط
fierce	ものすごく恐しい顔付きの	قوي ، مفترس
filter	フィルター	مصفاة
firefighter	消防士	رجل إطفاء
flame	炎	لهب
flowing	流れるような	جريان
flue	煙管	مُسرب ، مدخنة
fluid	流動体	سائل
foodstuff	栄養素	مادة غذائية
to forage	食糧をあさる	ينهب ، يطوف بحثاً عن العلف أو الطعام
to forecast	予報する	يتنبأ ، يتكهن (بحالة الجو)
to foresee	先見する	يتنبـأ بـ ، يتوقع أو يدرك قبل الحدوث
forklift	フォークリフト	الرافعة المشعّبة : رافعة ذات أصابع فولاذية تُقحم تحت الحمل
formulae	公式(複)	صيغة ، غذاء بديل عن اللبن (لتغذية الطفل)
foundry	鋳込み	مسبوكات ، مسبك المعادن
fragile	弱い	سهل المكسر ، هش
to function	働く	يؤدي (عملاً معيناً)
galaxy	銀河	المجرّة
gaseous	ガス状の	غازي
gene	遺伝子	الجينة ، المورّثة
genetics	遺伝学	علم الوراثة
genus	膝(複)	جنس ، طبقة
geological	地質学の	جيولوجي : خاص أو متعلق بعلم طبقات الأرض
geomorphic	地球の形の	جيومورفي : خاص بشكل الأرض أو سمات سطحها
geothermal	地熱の	حراري أرضي
germ	微生物	ميكروب ، جرثومة

ENGLISH	JAPANESE	ARABIC
gland	腺	غُدّة
glucose	ぶどう糖	الغلوكوز : سكّر العنب ، سكر النشاء
graph	グラフ	شيء مكتوب أو مرسوم
gravity	引力	جاذبية الأرض
grid	方眼	المِصْبَعة : شبكة قضبان مُتصالبة
to grow	育てる	ينمو ، ينبت
guessing	推量	تخمين ، حزر
gutters	樋	مزاريب ، قنوات
habit	習性	عادة
habitat	生息地	الموطن : بيئة الحيوان أو النبات
to harden	硬化する	يُقَسّي
harmful	有害な	مُؤذٍ ، ضار
hawk	タカ	صقر
hazard	危険、冒険	مخاطرة
headache	頭痛	صُداع
health	健康	ازدهار ، صحة
heartbeat	心拍	نبضة قلب
hectare	ヘクタール	الهكتار : عشرة آلاف متر مربع
helix	螺旋	لولب ، حافة الاذن الخارجية
hemisphere	地球の半球	نصف الكرة
hemophilia	血友病	المزاج النزفي : نزعة وراثية إلى النزف الدموي
high-pressure	高圧の	ضغط عالٍ
history	歴史	تاريخ
hollow	うつろな	مُجَوَّف
homogeneity	同種	تجانُس
homosexuality	同性愛	اللواطة
horizontal	水平の	أفقي
hormone	ホルモン	الهرمون
housekeeper	家計を切りもりする人	مدبِّرة المنزل
humid	湿気のある	رطب
hybrid	混血種	مُوَلَّد ، هجين
hydroelectric	水力発電の	كهربيمائي : متعلق بتوليد الكهرباء من القوة المائية
hydrogen	水素	الهيدروجين
hydrostatic	流体静力学の	هيدروستاتي : متعلق بتوازن الموائع وضغطها
hypertension	高血圧（症）	فرط ضغط الدم
hypoglycemia	低血糖（症）	نقص السكر
hypothesis	仮説	الفرضية
idiomatic	慣用語法の	فردي ، اصطلاحي
idiopathic	独特の	فردي ، ذاتي العلّة : ناشيء عفوياً أو عن علّة غامضة
illusion	幻影	وهـم
imagery	像	تخيّلات
to imagine	想像する	يتخيل
imitation	模倣	تقليد
immensity	巨大	ضخامة
imperfection	不完全	نقص ، عيب
inanimate	生命のない	لاحي ، غير ذي حياة
increment	増加	زيادة
indigestible	消化しにくい	عسِر الهضم
infection	伝染	تلوّث ، عدوى
infestation	浸入	ابتلاء
inflexible	変えられない	صلب ، لا ينثني
infrared	赤外線の	دون الأحمر
ingestion	摂取する	استيعاب
inheritance	相続	ميراث ، أرث
to injure	傷つける	يجرح
to inspect	検査する	يفحص ، يفتش
insulator	絶縁体	العازل
insulin	インシュリン	الأنسولين
intensity	強烈さ	كثافة ، شدة
intercourse	交通関係	اتصال ، جماع
interfere	邪魔をする	يتدخل
intravenously	静脈内に	مُدخل عن طريق الأوردة
to invade	入り込む	يغزو ، يجتاح

ENGLISH	JAPANESE	ARABIC
inversion	発明	عكس
invisible	見分けにくい	خفي ، غير منظور
in vitro	ガラス器内での	خارج الجسم الحي ، في أنبوب اختبار
ionizing	電離すること	تأين ، تحويل إلى أيونات
irregularity	不規則	الشذوذية
irritability	刺激に敏感なこと	التأثرية قبول الاثارة ، التهيّجيّة
isotope	アイソトープ	النظير
to jettison	捨てる	يتخلص من ، يطرح
kidney	腎臓	كلية
kingdom	王国	المملكة
laboratory	実験室	مختبر
laser	レーザー	اللازر ، أداة لتضخيم اشعاع الترددات ضمن منطقة النور المنظور
latitude	緯度	خط العرض
layer	層	طبقة
length	長さ	طـول
lens	レンズ	عدسة
to lessen	少くする	يُقَلّل
levitation	浮揚	سباحة في الهواء
liberation	解放	محرر
lifespan	寿命	عمر : حياة المرء على الأرض
lifetime	生涯	العمر : حياة المرء أو مداها
limb	縁辺	وصل ، طرف
limestone	石灰岩	حجر الكلس
lineaments	特徴	أسارير ، قسمات
lipid	脂質	دهن
lithium	リチウム	الليثيوم
locality	産地	المحلّية : كون الشيء محلياً
logic	論理	منطق ، علم المنطق
lung	肺	رئة
lysine	リジン	حامض أميني
majority	大多数	الأكثرية ، الأغلبية
malfunction	機能不全	قصور
malnutrition	栄養不良	سوء التغذية
mammalia	ほ乳綱	ذوات الأثداء
manganese	マンガン	المنغيز
to manipulate	操作する	يتلاعب بـ ، يؤثر في
manual	手動の	يدوي
to manufacture	製造業者	يصنع
mathematics	数学	رياضي
to maximize	最大化する	يزيد إلى الحد الأعلى
meaningless	無意味な	خلو من المعنى أو المغزى
measurement	測定	القياس
mechanic	機械的な	ميكانيكي ، الصانع اليدوي
medication	薬物処理	معالجة
mercury	水銀	زئبق
metabolism	新陳代謝	مجموع العمليات المتصلة بناء الدوتوبلازما و دثورها
metallic	金属性の	معدني
meteorologist	気象学者	الأرصادي ، العالم بالأرصاد الجوية
microelectronics	マイクロエレクトロニクス	اليكترونيات مجهرية
microscope	顕微鏡	(الميكروسكوب ، المجهر)
microwave	マイクロ波	الموجة الصغرى : موجة كهرطيسية قصيرة جداً
mineral	鉱物	معدن
to minimize	最小化する	يخفض إلى الحد الأدنى
to modify	改良する	يعدل ، يخفف
module	モジュール	وحدة قياس
mold	鋳型	قالب ، عفن ، تراب وبخاصة ثرى ناعم غني بالمادة العضوية
molecule	分子	الجزيىء
mosquito	蚊	بعوضة
mud	泥	وحل ، طين
mule	らば	بغل
multiple	多数の	مُرَكّب ، مضاعف ، متعدد
multispectral	多スペクタル感応性の	ذو مجالات متعددة
multitude	多数	متعدد

ENGLISH	JAPANESE	ARABIC
muscle	筋肉	عضـلة
myelin	ミリエン	النخاعين
nacelle	つりかご	كنّة المحرك : حجرة مقفلة في طائرة خاصة بالمحرك وقد تفرد أحياناً للملاحين
narrative	物語	قصة ، سرد الأخبار
natural gas	天然ガス	الغاز الطبيعي
nautical	航海の	بحري : متعلق بالبحارة أو السفن
navigation	航行	ابحار ، ملاحة
neon	ネオン	مصباح تفريغ أنبوبي الشكل يكون فيه الغاز ، غاز النيون ، محتوياً على مقدار كبير من النيون
neuter	中性	ليس بالمذكر ولا بالمؤنث ، حيادي
neutral	中性の	محايد
nickel	ニッケル	النيكل ، النكلة : قطعة نقدية قيمتها خمس سنتات
nitric	窒素の	نتريك : محتوٍ على نتروجين خماسي التكافؤ
nitrogen	窒素	النتروجين
nocturnal	夜の	ليلّ ، ناشط في الليل
non-prescription	医者の処方せんなしで買える	وصفة غير طبّية
normotensive	正常血圧の	(شخص) ذو ضغط دم عادي أو طبيعي
nozzle	管先	الأنف
nuclear	核の	نَووي
nylon	ナイロン	النيلون
obesity	肥満	بدانة
obscure	暗い	غامض
observation	観視すること	مراقبة ، ملاحظة
oceanographer	海洋学	الأوقيانوغرافي : العالم بالمحيطات
offshore	沖合の	بعيداً عن الشاطيء
oilshale	油母頁岩	الطين المحتوي على النفط
opaque	不透明体	المعتمة : مادة ملوّنة تستعمل لتعتيم ، جزء من الصورة السلبية ، مبهم
ophthalmologist	眼科医	طبيب العيون
oral	口で行う	متعلق بالفم ، شفهي
organism	有機物	الكائن الحي
origin	起始点	نشوء ، الأصل
ornithologist	鳥類学者	العالم بالطيور
outpost	最先端	مركز أو نقطة الحدود
overactive	あまり活動しすぎる	مفرط النشاط
oversimplification	極度の単純化	تبسيط شديد
overweight	重すぎる	أثقل من الضروري أو المسموح به
oxide	オキシデート	أكسيد
oxygen	酸素	الأكسجين
pain	痛み	الألم
parachute	パラシュート	مظلّة
parasite	寄生するもの	الطُفيلي ، حيوان أو نبات متطفل على حيوان أو نبات آخر
particulates	微粒子	دقائق
pathogenic	病源の	مسبب مرضاً ، ممرض
penicillin	ペニシリン	البنيسيلين : عقار مضاد للجراثيم
penumbra	半影部	شبه الظل
percentage	パーセント	نسبة مئوية
perception	知覚	القدرة على الفهم ، الادراك الحي
to perch	座る	يحط الطائر
periodically	定期的に	دورياً
peripheral	周辺の	محيطي : متعلق بمحيط ، سطحي ، خارجي
perpendicular	垂直	عمودي
petri dish	シャーレ	صحن زجاجي صغير رقيق ذو غطاء مرن يستعمل بخاصة في المختبرات لزرع البكتيريا
petrochemical	石油化学製品	المادة البتروكيميائية
petroleum	石油	البترول ، النفط
phenomena	事象	واقعة أو حادثة قابلة للوصف والتفسير العلمين ، ظاهرة
phosphate	リン酸塩	الفوسفات
phosphorus	リン	فسفوري
photochemical	光化学物質	كيميائي ضوئي
photon	光子	الفوتون : وحدة الكم الضوئي
photosphere	光球	سطح الشمس النيّر ، كرة ضوئية

ENGLISH	JAPANESE	ARABIC
photosynthesis	光合成の	التخليق أو التركيب الضوئي
photovoltaic	光電池の	كهربائي ضوئي
phylum	門	الشعبة (في تصنيف الحيوان والنبات)
physically	身体上	جسدياً
physician	内科医	الطبيب
physics	物理学	الفيزياء
physiology	生理学	الفيسيولوجيا : علم وظائف الأعضاء
pilot	パイロット	القائد ، الدليل
planet	惑星	نجم ، كوكب سيّار
plasmid	プラスミド	بلازما
plywood	合板	الخشب الرقائقي
poison	毒	سُمّ
polarity	極性	القطبية ، الاستقطابية
political	政治に関する	سياسي
pollen	花粉	غبار الطلع ، لقاح
pollutant	汚染物	الملوّن
polymer	ポリマー	البوليمر : مركب كيميائي يُشكل بالبَلْمَرُ
population	人口	السُّكان
portion	部分	قسم ، جزء
positron	陽電子	البوزترون : جُسيم موجب ذو كتلة تعادل كتلة الالكترون
precarious	不安定な	متفلفل
precaution	用心	احتراس
pregnancy	妊娠	حمل
prematurely	尚早に	ولادة قبل الأوان
prescription	処方せん	وصفة طبيّة
prevention	防止	منع
procedure	手続き	البروتوكول ، إجراء
process	プロセス	عملية
prognosis	予後	التكهن
projectile	発射できる	قذيفة
promising	見込みのある	ينتظر له مستقبل مرموق
prone	うつぶせの	عرضة لـ ، ميّال أو نزّاع إلى
propane	プロパン	غاز بروبين
protein	蛋白質	البروتين
proton	陽子	البروتون ، جسيم يحمل وحدة من الكهربائية الموجبة ويشكل جزءاً من الذرة
protozoan	原生動物	البَرْزوي
proximity	近いこと	قرب (في المكان أو الزمان)
pulse rate	脈拍数	معدل النبض
to purify	精化する	يُطهر
quantity	量	كمية
quartz	石英	المَرْو ، الكوارتز
to radiate	放射する	يُشِعّ
radioactive	放射能のある	إشعاعي النشاط
radium	ラディウム	الراديوم : عنصر فلزي اشعاعي النشاط
radon	ラドン	الرادون ، غاز الرادون
rapid	早い	سريع
ray	射出	شعاع
reaction	反応	رد فعل ، تفاعل
reattachment	再逮捕	إعادة وصل
recognition	承認	تمييز ، تعرف
recombinant	遺伝子間組換えの	اعادة مزج
to reconstruct	復元する	يبني أو ينظم من جديد
to recoup	埋めあわせをする	يعوض ، يسترد ، يستعيد
to regenerate	回生させる	يشكل نسيجاً أو عضواً جديداً يحل محل نسيج أو عضومفقود ، يجدد
relationship	関係	علاقة ، قرابة
renal	腎臓の	كلوي : ذو علاقة بالكليتين
reproduction	生殖	انتاج ، تكاثر ، نسخة طبق الأصل
reptile	爬虫類	من الزواحف ، الزاحف
reputation	世評	شهرة ، سمعة
research	研究	بحث ، البحث العلمي
resin	樹脂	الرّاتينْج : مادة صمغية تسيل من معظم الأشجار عند قطعها او جرحها

ENGLISH	JAPANESE	ARABIC
to resist	負けない	يقاوم
respiration	呼吸	تنفّس
responsibility	責任	مسؤولية
responsive	応答的な	سريع الاستجابة ، مستجيب
to restrict	制限する	يحدّ ، يُقيد
results	結果	نتائج
to retard	進行を防げる	يؤخّر ، يُعوق
retina	網膜	الشبكيّة ، شبكية العين
to reverse	逆にする	يعكس ، يقلب
revolution	変革	الدوران ، طواف جرم سماوي في مدار
risk	危険	مخاطرة
robot	ロボット	الرُّبوط : إنسان أتوماتيكي أوآلي
rocket	ロケット	قنبلة أو قذيفة صاروخية
to ruin	破滅する	يخرّب ، يدمّر
saccharin	サッカリン	السُّكرين : مركب متبلر أحلى من قصب السكر مئات المرات
salmon	サケ	السّلمون
to scatter	四散させる	يفرّق ، يبعثر
scholar	学者	عالم
science	科学	علم
scurvy	壊血病	الأسقربوط : داء من أعراضه تورّم اللثة ونزف الدم منها
sea level	海面	مستوى سطح البحر
secretion	分泌（液）	إفراز
seismograph	震動記録	المرخّة : مرْسمة الزلازل
self-generating	自生	توليد ذاتي
self-limiting	自ら制限した	تحديد ذاتي
self-supporting	自給している	كاف نفسه بنفسه
self-sustaining	自給している	معيل نفسه بنفسه
sensory	知覚の	حسي : ذو علاقة بالاحساس
serious	重大な	جدّي
sex-linked	伴性の	ذو علاقة بالجنس
shallow	浅い	ضحل ، قليل العمق
shark	鮫	القرش : سمك مُفترس
silicon	ケイ素	السّليكوون : مركب سليكوني عضوي
simultaneous	同時の	متزامن ، حادث في وقت واحد
skull	頭骨	جمجمة ، عقل
slide rule	計算尺	المسطرة الحاسبة
smog	スモッグ	الضّبخن : مزيج من ضباب ودخان
smokestack	煙突	مدخنة
to sneeze	くしゃみをする	يعطس
sodium	ナトリウム	الصوديوم
solar	太陽の	شمسي
solidified	凝固、結晶した	متجمّد ، متصلّب
soluble	溶解できる	ذوّاب : قابل للذوبان في سائل
solvent	溶剤	المذيب : مادة مذيبة
sonic	音の	صوتي
sophisticated	洗練された	مغشوش ، متكلّف ، محرّف
source	源	مصدر
spacecraft	宇宙船	السفينة الفضائية
spatial	空間の	فضائي ، مكاني
specimen	標本	عيّنة ، نموذج
spectrometer	分光計	مقياس الطيف
spectroscopy	分光学	المطيافة : التحليل الطيفي باستخدام المطياف
sphygmomanometer	血圧計	المضغاط : أداة لقياس ضغط الدم الشرياني بخاصة
spinal	背骨の	فقري ، شوكي
spiral	螺旋形の	لولبي ، حلزوني
stable	安定性のある	إسطبل
statistics	統計学	إحصائي
steam	水蒸気	بخار
steroid	ステロイド	مركب الستيرويد
stimulus	刺激	الحاضر ، المنبّه
strata	層	طبقات ، أطوار
straw	わら	قش
structure	構造	تركيب ، بنية

ENGLISH	JAPANESE	ARABIC
subclass	亜綱	فـرع رئيسي (من طبقة)
sub-genus	亜属	الجُنَيس (في تصنيف الحيوان أو النبات)
to submerge	水中に入れる	يَغمُر
subphylum	亜門	الأُمَيمة (في تصنيف الاحياء)
subsonic	亜音速の	دون (أو أقل) من سرعة الصوت
subspecies	亜種	النُويع (في منتصف الأحياء)
substance	内容	جوهر ، مادة
substitute	代理	البديل
subtitle	サブタイトル	عنوان فرعي
sulfite	亜硫酸塩·	كبريت
sulfuric	硫黄の	كبريتي
sunspot	黒点	كلفة الشمس : احدى كلف الشمس وهي بقع داكنة تبدو بين فترة وأخرى على سطح الشمس
superbly	壮麗に	ببروعة
surgeon	外科医	الجَرّاح : الطبيب الجَرّاح
sweetener	甘味料	مُحلّي
systolic	心収縮の	انقباضي
talon	爪	مُخلَب ، إصبع الانسان أو يده
technician	専門技術者	الفني : الاختصاصي بالدقائق التقنية لموضوع أوحرفة ما
telescope	望遠鏡	التِلِسكوب
tension	緊張	تَوتُر
terrestrial	陸上の	أحد سكان الأرض ، أرضي
territory	領域	منطقة ، أقليم
test tube	試験管	أنبوب الاختبار
therapy	療法	مداواة
thermocouple	熱電対	المزدوجة الحرارية
thermometer	温度計	ميزان الحرارة
thrombosis	血栓症	الخَثر : تكوُّن الجلطة أو وجودها في الوعاء الدموي
thyrotoxicosis	甲状腺中毒症	ثايروتوكسيكوسيس
tomography	断層撮影	الرسم السطحي أو الطبقي (بأشعة إكس)
topaz	トパーズ	التوباز : حجر كريم مختلف الأشكال والالوان
topmost	一番高い	الأعلى
transplant	移殖	ازدراع
treatment	処置	معاملة ، معالجة
tremor	身震い	ارتعاش
trench	掘割り	خندق
tumor	腫れ物	ورم ، ورم خبيث
turbojet	ターボジェット	النفاثة التربينية : طائرة مزودة بمحركات تربينية نفاثة
turbulence	乱流	تمرد ، اضطراب
ulcer	潰瘍	قَرحة
unborn	まだ生まれていない	لم يولد بعد ، مُقبِل
unconsciousness	無意識	اللا شعور ، اللا وعي
uncontaminated	汚れていない	غير مُلوَّث
unconventional	因襲にとらわれない	غير تقليدي
uninhabited	禁じられていない	غير مأهول بالسكان ، غير مسكون
universe	全世界	الكون
unreachable	手の届かない	غير ممكن الوصول اليه
uranium	ウラン	اليورانيوم
urine	尿	بَول
vaccination	予防接種	تَلقيح
variant	変種	مُتَنوع
verification	検証	التثبت من ، التحقق من
vertebrate	脊椎動物	الفقاري : حيوان من الفقاريات
vertical	垂直の	عمودي
to vibrate	振動する	يهز ، يذبذب
volcano	火山 (口)	بركان
to vomit	吐く	يلفظ ، يتقيأ
watt-hour	ワット時	الواط الساعي
wavelength	波長	الطول الموجي
to weld	溶接する	يَلحُم
whale shark	ジンベイザメ	حوت قرشي
to whiten	白くする	يبيض
windmill	風車	الهليكوبتر ، الطاحونة الهوائية

ENGLISH	JAPANESE	ARABIC
windshield	風防	حاجب الريح : الحاجب الزجاجية
x-ray	X 線	الأشعة السينية : أشعة إكس
zinc	亜鉛	الزّنك ، الخارصين : عضو فلزي أبيض مزرق
zone	一帯	منطقة ، المنطقة الكروية